HOLY EROS

RECOVERING THE PASSION OF GOD

HOLY EROS

RECOVERING THE PASSION OF GOD

James D. Whitehead
Evelyn Eaton Whitehead

ORBIS BOOKS
Maryknoll, New York 10545

Founded in 1970, Orbis Books endeavors to publish works that enlighten the mind, nourish the spirit, and challenge the conscience. The publishing arm of the Maryknoll Fathers and Brothers, Orbis seeks to explore the global dimensions of the Christian faith and mission, to invite dialogue with diverse cultures and religious traditions, and to serve the cause of reconciliation and peace. The books published reflect the views of their authors and do not represent the official position of the Maryknoll Society. To learn more about Maryknoll and Orbis Books, please visit our website at www.maryknollsociety.org.

Library of Congress Cataloging-in-Publication Data

Whitehead, James D.
  Holy eros : recovering the passion of God / James D. Whitehead, Evelyn Eaton Whitehead.
      p. cm.
  Includes bibliographical references and index.
  ISBN 978-1-57075-813-3
  1. Love—Religious aspects—Christianity. 2. God
(Christianity)—Love. 3. God (Christianity)—Worship and love. 4.
Spirituality. 5. Christian life. I. Whitehead, Evelyn Eaton. II.
Title.
  BV4639.W465 2009
  241'.4—dc22
                                        2008019804

For
Maureen and John Reid
Molly and Tom Reid

honoring lives of eros and grace

"To explore again the profound interpenetration
of eros and the spiritual life.
This terribly fraught arena in Western Christendom,
where the sexual meets the spiritual,
urgently awaits the discovery of new paths to God."

—Philosopher Charles Taylor, recipient of the prestigious
2007 Templeton Prize for Progress in Research on Religion,
in his acclaimed book *A Secular Age*, p. 767

Contents

Introduction: The Spiritual Search Today   1

PART ONE
THE MARRIAGE OF EROS AND GRACE

1. *Naming Eros*
   Claiming the Energies of Life   9

2. *Naming Grace*
   Receiving God's Blessing and Favor   19

3. *Discovering Our God of Passion and Extravagance*   30

4. *A Spirituality of Eros*
   Praying for Our Heart's Desire   42

PART TWO
THE BODY'S ROMANCE WITH EROS

5. *Eros in Everyday Life*
   Sensuality, Emotion, Sexuality   53

6. *Benefits of the Body*
   Storehouse of Wisdom and Energy   64

7. *Befriending Our Bodies*
   Lovely, Limited, Holy   77

8. *The Eros of Pleasure*
   Pathway to Presence and Gratitude   89

PART THREE

Unexpected Pathways to Eros

9. *Eros of Hope*
   Uninvited Envoy from Another World   99

10. *Eros of Suffering*
    Energy to Resist and to Accept   108

11. *Eros of Anger*
    Resource for Social Transformation   119

12. *Eros of Compassion*
    Passion's Bridge to Justice   131

PART FOUR

The Rhythms of Eros

13. *Presence and Absence*
    Honoring Light and Darkness   143

14. *Holding On and Letting Go*
    Learning the Rules of Engagement   153

15. *Feasting and Fasting*
    Nourishing the Spirit   161

16. *Shadows of Eros*
    Vital Energy Gone Astray   168

Conclusion: The Eros of the Gift   177

Additional Resources   185

Bibliography   197

Index   207

INTRODUCTION

The Spiritual Search Today

Spirituality is our response to the living reality of God. This Divine Mystery is revealed to us—quite literally "takes flesh" for us as Christians—in the person of Jesus. The reality of God continues to embrace us through God's Spirit, everywhere active among us and in history—sustaining us, causing us to hope, serving as the source of our own commitments of creativity, compassion, and justice in God's world.

Christian spirituality is shaped by the stories and symbols of the biblical tradition. The Bible describes God's Spirit not in the abstract categories of philosophy but in the earlier—and earthier—Hebrew language of *ruah* or breath. This image evokes the intimacy of God—as immediate to us as our own breathing; as essential as oxygen; as resonant with our longings as a sigh or a groan. The faith community is the gathering of those who, empowered by the Spirit of God, strive to live in ways that reverence this mysterious presence and its saving purpose for all creation. By word and sacrament this community nourishes each of us in our common call to share in the mission of Jesus, giving witness to God's empowering love for the world.

But, as theologian Margaret Miles reminds us, the spiritual traditions of Western Christianity have been influenced by two fundamental assumptions that are at odds with this biblical worldview. The first: a separate spiritual realm exists that is vastly superior to the ordinary world of human life. The second: our religious task is to disengage ourselves from involvement with the people and

1

events of this world, so that we may participate more fully in the spiritual realm. These assumptions find their roots not in the gospels but in the dualisms of Western philosophical thought—body vs. soul, passion vs. reason, *eros* vs. *agape*.

Familiar religious attitudes continue to reflect this antagonism. We have come to regard spirituality as the realm of the sacred, to be sought as a haven from the cares and responsibilities of the secular world. We have learned that spirituality connects us with a supernatural realm that is immensely more valuable than our ordinary life. We have been taught that the spirit seeks release from our "lower nature," the demands and needs of the body. Understanding spirituality in this way still makes sense to many people, who find their own lives accurately reflected in these tensions. But, increasingly, Christians find this opposition less familiar, even false to their experience of grace.

Many people of faith today seek a worldly spirituality. We long to bring our daily existence—its apparent ordinariness as well as its flashpoints of crisis and consolation—in touch with what is most real: God's Spirit alive in our lives and in our world. The spiritual search today seeks out more significant ways to connect with the world, both to raise up the simple pleasures that bring authentic delight and to face up to the complex issues that carry the prophetic agenda of our own time.

A WIDER HUMAN HUNGER

Spirituality is not limited to Christian experience. Throughout history the wisdom traditions of the world have awakened human hearts to the spiritual. And people today in many places and with diverse backgrounds explicitly acknowledge spirituality as a significant dimension of their lives; they speak of their spiritual quest or view life as a spiritual journey. For many, this journey is supported by the beliefs and practices of a particular religious heritage—Judaism, Buddhism, Islam, Christianity. But many others report, often insistently: "I am a spiritual person, but I am not religious." Sometimes this statement is made apologetically, but often it's made in anger and even resentment. There is a sense that the organized religious group I grew up in has somehow let me down. Or that many of the beliefs inherited from my religious tradition are no longer credible. Somehow, what I have known as "religion" doesn't honor the complexities of my own journey of light and darkness, of belief and unbelief. But even as people turn away from their earlier religious settings, many find themselves bereft—recognizing that a deeply insistent part of the soul still longs for nourishment.

Across today's world, millions continue to embrace the symbols and beliefs of a particular religion or spiritual tradition as authentic expression of their own religiousness. But many contemporary seekers express their religiousness differently. Some may draw symbols and practices from several spiritual traditions; others look outside all formal religious traditions to symbols from nature or art or science. But in all these expressions, the spiritual journey expresses a search for something larger than *self* in which to place our trust...and the struggle to live in faithful contact with this transforming reality.

Scholars today—social scientists as well as theologians—suggest that our hunger for contact with the foundational source of significance is part of what it means to be human. Even those who shy away from identifying such longing as *religious* recognize this spiritual sensitivity as a widespread human characteristic. Still, most would suggest that there is no "generic" spirituality. Our hunger for meaning, our awareness of transcendence, our experience of the sacred—these find expression in a specific language, in particular symbols, in concrete practices.

This book will examine the spiritual resources—rooted in language, symbols, practices—of the Christian tradition that support the spiritual search today.

THE SPIRITUAL SEARCH TODAY

Today's spiritual search looks more deeply into our everyday experiences of family life and work and public involvement. These familiar settings offer our most immediate opportunity to respond to the needs of the world. More profoundly, we recognize these encounters as sacred space, the places where we most regularly find God . . . or perhaps better, where God finds us.

Increasingly today, Christians seek human flourishing—the practical well-being of the human community now—as a gospel-inspired goal. We recognize constructive participation in our society's life as part of the Christian vocation. Stewardship of the earth and service to its people are embraced as religious commitments. Through these actions, we help make real God's promise of humanity transformed in grace.

Contemporary spirituality continues to draw strength from the witness of Christian communities throughout centuries of faith. But for many Christians today, spirituality is rooted less in a stable religious identity and more in an unfolding relationship with God, a relationship marked by the developments and uncertainties and surprises that come with a deepening intimacy. Spirituality, then, is less a 'state of soul' and more an embrace of the Divine Mystery.

Many who live religiously committed lives today do not base their spirituality primarily on the credibility of particular theological doctrines. Instead, their spirituality reflects a greater mindfulness of the enduring questions that surround the experience of human life. Religious leaders recognize this shift in spiritual sensitivity. The U.S. Catholic bishops, for example, have acknowledged that "we are in need of a new symbolic and affective system" if the churches are to respond to the spiritual longing of our time. Fresh and compelling images, rich in emotional resonance, will be required to express both the hunger and the hope that inspire the spiritual journey today.

Among theologians, too, there is greater awareness of the ultimate mystery of the universe and of our existence. This awareness is registered in an increasing modesty. Traditional formulations of religious belief have, perhaps, claimed to know too much: the concepts are too full, too clear, too certain. But "God" is not a problem to be solved or a theory to be proved by discursive reason. Theology today is more tentative, recognizing that its grasp of divine reality is partial. Its interpretations of the symbols of sacred transcendence must remain open to both purification and development.

The spiritual search today is grounded in an awareness of the mysterious Presence at the heart of the world. This presence comes as gift, with a power that creates, sustains, reconciles, and heals. It is a presence that engages us personally, leading humanity beyond narrow self-interest into fuller participation in life. It is a presence that defies simple definition, but as theologian Michael Himes reminds us, the "least inadequate" way we have to describe this presence is as radical love.

Christian thinkers today, Pope Benedict XVI and philosopher Charles Taylor among them, are returning to the ancient image of *eros* as an apt symbol of God's radical love. This is an *eros* known through and beyond sexual arousal; its vital energy courses through the world, enlivening and healing human hearts. Experienced as affection and also as compassion, in desire and also in hope, *eros* becomes ever more generous as it folds into that most capacious love described in the Bible as *agape*.

This book explores the cultivation of *eros*. Our approach follows theologian Karl Rahner's directive: to recover and to overcome. We will return to the ancient image of *eros* to recover its potential to reveal God's action among us today; we will acknowledge the biases against body, sexuality, and desire that have found their way into the Christian tradition and must now be overcome. In dialogue with a range of contemporary authors—social scientists, theologians, spiritual writers—we will examine the interplay among passion, pleasure, justice, and transformation. The goal of our endeavor is, finally, to recover the confidence expressed by St. Irenaeus: "The glory of God is a human person fully alive."

PART ONE

THE MARRIAGE OF EROS AND GRACE

The human journey is sustained by
eros and grace.

Eros names the vital energy that animates
all of creation.

Eros lies at the source of our desires—
for friendship and love, for fruitful work, for life in abundance.

Grace names the healing energy that flows from our loving God,
transforming the world through compassion and hope.

Eros and grace embrace in the heart of God;
yet often they are divorced in our lives.

In Part One
we explore the human hunger to bring together in harmony
the vital energies of eros and grace.

1

Naming Eros

CLAIMING THE ENERGIES OF LIFE

Eros burns at the heart of our sexuality,
fueling every passionate engagement with life.

Our God is a God of life—of exuberant, surprising, extravagant vitality. Creation testifies to the overflowing energy of God's presence in our world. Our own generosity, our surprising ability to forgive, and our endless desire for more life all witness to this God-given energy within us. *Eros*, once used to identify a god in ancient Greece, now serves as a metaphor that names the vital energy Christians recognize as God's gift.

NAMING EROS

- *Eros is the vital energy that courses through the world, animating every living thing. It is the force that turns the flower to the sun, the energy that stirs humans to be in touch, to reach out and link their lives in lasting ways. Eros is the raw energy that impels an infant to seize a bright marble lying in the dirt and put it into her mouth. Eros wants to touch, to taste, and even to consume.*

- *Eros is the force that quickens our hearts when we encounter suffering and moves us to help and heal. Sex, curiosity,*

9

compassion—Eros moves through our lives in delightful and bewildering ways. To live a responsible life we will have to name and even tame this ambiguous force.

- *Eros is our desire for closeness, the visceral hope that moves us out of solitude and motivates us to chance the risky relationships of friendship and love. Eros is about union— with the beautiful other, with a suffering person, with the world of nature waiting to be embraced and protected.*

- *Eros finds expression in our longing to close the gap between ourselves and others, our yearning to be joined to our heart's desire. Theologian James Nelson describes eros as "the yearning for fulfillment and deep connection, . . . the divine-human energy, a drive toward union with that to which we belong."*

Longing adds to desire the note of absence: a lover lost, a hope still on the horizon, an ideal that remains at large. *Eros* was Augustine's longing as he prayed, "Our hearts are restless, O God, and they do not rest until they rest in you." As longing, *eros* registers the absence that lurks in every human presence. In the midst of every embrace, however intense and promising, we fear that this coming together cannot endure. Our lover and we ourselves are sure to perish; how will our love last?

We recognize *eros* most dramatically when it drains from our lives. In *The Noonday Demon,* the impassioned story of his own struggle with depression, Andrew Solomon writes, "The opposite of depression is not happiness, but vitality." Depression deprives us of our vitality, our ability to be fully present to our lives in their delights and distresses. In seasons of depression, it seems that the vital energy of *eros* has deserted us, leaving us bereft.

In depression, enthusiasm departs as we lose interest in the world. The agonizing experience of depression carries a lesson of great importance. This energy does not belong to us; it is not ours to possess. The vitality of *eros* is not a birthright, but a gift and a grace.

Eros is the traditional name given to the body's desire and delight. *Eros* entered the Western imagination through Greek mythology. In the classic tales, *Eros* was the name of the youngest of the deities, irresistible and fair, who subdued the hearts of both gods and humans. Earlier Greek creation stories had cast *eros* as more than the god of sensual love. *Eros* was a cosmic force, the power that had drawn the universe out of chaos, bringing together the disparate elements of reality to form the human world. The original meaning of the term *eros*, then, extended well beyond the sexual.

In these early myths, *eros* represented a dynamic life-giving energy with both creative and destructive potential. While providing the essential vitality of life, the force of *eros* could also consume and destroy. Even as *eros* was honored as a divine gift, it was recognized as a source of madness. A life without *eros* would be cold and empty, but the untamed passion of desire could also drive a person insane.

When Jewish scholars translated the Hebrew texts into Greek, they faced the question of how to translate the Bible's many stories of sensual affection and erotic love. They knew that Eros named a god, but this was not their God. Thus the word *eros* does not appear in either the Hebrew Scriptures or the Greek New Testament—with one exception.

In the book of Proverbs we are introduced to a married woman "whose feet do not stay at home." She invites a man, "Come, let us take our fill of love until morning, let us delight ourselves with love [*eros*], for my husband is not at home" (Prov 7:18–19). In its sole appearance in the Bible, *eros* was identified with adulterous passion.

THE LANGUAGE OF LOVE IN THE BIBLE

The reality of *eros* as the vital energy that animates creation is not absent from scripture. But this volatile force, its reputation already compromised by the many myths in the surrounding Greek culture, often appears in disguise.

The Song of Songs is the most erotic book in the Bible. But even here, as biblical translators sought a vocabulary for love, they avoided the term *eros*. Instead, they selected another Greek work—*agape*—to name the lovers' sensual delight and physical affection in this sacred poem.

> His eyes are like doves beside springs of water...
> His body is ivory work, encrusted with sapphires.
> His legs are alabaster columns...
> His speech is most sweet and
> He is altogether desirable. (Song 5:12, 14–15, 16)

This poem celebrates the couple's passionate affection with no mention of children and little reference to marriage. The lovers praise one another's physical beauty and delight in each other's presence. Their relationship is profoundly mutual, and often the woman initiates the erotic exchange.

Over the centuries, this highly erotic text confounded both Jewish and Christian scholars. Its imagery, so charged with sexual connotations, made many uncomfortable, but since its author was understood to be the great king Solomon, the religious community felt compelled to accept the text.

If the text were to be revered, special interpretation would be required. Perhaps, it was suggested, the sexual imagery was an allegory for the powerful love between God and the human soul. The poem could be redeemed by understanding its true focus as spiritual devotion, not the sweaty, passionate affection of two human lovers. So began the tradition of "spiritualizing" the erotic impact of this text. Eventually Christian mystics such as John of the Cross and Teresa of Avila returned to sexual imagery to express the love between humans and God. But such erotic piety remained at the periphery of a Western tradition that favored a dichotomy between sensuality and spirituality.

Sex and sensuality play a central role in the biblical story of Ruth, a woman who found favor with God. Ruth was a Moabite who was married to a Jewish man. After his death, Ruth—as a woman, a foreigner, and a childless widow—was the ultimate outsider, but her mother-in-law Naomi befriended her and took her to Israel. A bond of affection deepened between the two women, as celebrated in Ruth's vow to Naomi: "Where you go I will go; where you live I will live. Your people will be my people and your God my God. Where you die, I will die; there will I be buried" (Ruth 1:16–17).

In Israel, Ruth had to find a way to survive. Learning of the Jewish law that required landowners to leave some of their crop in the field so that the poor could glean the leftovers, she determined to find a landowner "in whose sight she might find favor." The text then wryly notes that "as it happened," Ruth found herself in the field of a wealthy man named Boaz. He noticed her, offered to protect her, and allowed her to glean grain from his fields. Ruth was startled by his kindness and directly questioned him. "Why have I found favor in your sight, that you should take notice of me . . . a foreigner?" (Ruth 2:10).

Then the erotic overtones of the story pick up. The text goes on to say that Naomi encouraged Ruth to go that evening to the threshing floor where Boaz and his crew were harvesting their crop. Naomi urged Ruth, "Wash and anoint yourself and put on your best clothes." She told Ruth to lie close to Boaz who, when he awoke in the morning, would be surprised (and happy!) to find her next to him. Ruth "found favor" with Boaz and "the Lord made her to conceive and bear a son" (Ruth 4:13). This son was the grandfather of King David and thus an ancestor of Jesus. The outsider Ruth found favor with Naomi and Boaz, and this "favor" from God bore fruit in the birth of a son. The phrase "to find favor" would become a common way of describing God's grace. In the story of Ruth, *eros* and grace embrace in surprising and fruitful ways.

EROS AND AGAPE

The New Testament writers also had to select words to describe human and divine love. Like their Jewish ancestors, these authors knew that the term *eros* had already been widely used in Greek mythology as the name of a god. With its connotations of passion and erotic delight, *eros* seemed not quite fitting for a religious text. They were left with two other words for love—*agape* and *philia*. In the famous passage in John's gospel, "God so loved the world that he gave his only-begotten son" (Jn 3:16), God's love is called *agape* in the Greek text; this term came to designate the inclusive love that the Creator and Jesus have for all humanity. In John 11, we read of Jesus' grief at the death of Lazarus, a person whom Jesus loved; here the author of the gospel chose the word *philia*. This word came to stand for the brotherly affection that Christians should show one another.

Although *eros* was absent from the New Testament, the early Greek-speaking theologians in the Eastern Church had no qualms about using the word to describe both God's love and human love. Gregory of Nyssa believed that "*Eros* translates better than *agape* the excess of love that the soul can have when its eyes are fixed upon the inaccessible beauty of the Divine nature." Origen used the term in a positive sense in his commentary on the Song of Songs. Pseudo-Dionysius in the fifth century wrote of the divine longing (*eros*) of God.

Meanwhile in the Western Church a more pessimistic vision of human passion developed. Theologians began to see an apparent dichotomy between the selfish earthly love of *eros* and the generous holy love of *agape*. Augustine's theology of original sin pointed to a profound brokenness in human nature, a brokenness that rendered all our passions unreliable. The reformers Luther and Calvin would take up this pessimistic view. Nothing in depraved human nature, they would argue, can lead us to God; grace alone suffices.

This interpretation of human nature framed the work of the twentieth-century Lutheran theologian Anders Nygren. In *Agape and Eros* Nygren describes *eros* as an essentially self-centered expression of human desire; *agape* names the total self-giving love of God. Nygren sees here a radical opposition: *eros* and *agape* represent two essentially different kinds of love. As

Sallie McFague notes, "Nygren's position rests on the worthlessness of human beings"; in the end, he sees *eros* as "the corruption of *agape*."

Nygren's work influenced several generations of Christian thinkers, becoming the standard interpretation adopted in both theological and pastoral writing. But by the 1950s Nygren's influence started to wane, as both Protestant (Paul Tillich) and Catholic (Martin D'Arcy) theologians began to challenge his deeply pessimistic view of erotic love.

RECLAIMING EROS

Many contemporary voices have joined this challenge. Pope Benedict XVI, in his first encyclical letter, *Deus Caritas Est* (God Is Love), offers a more optimistic Catholic vision of the complementarity of human and divine love. The letter does not begin with a review of doctrine but with a discussion of *eros*. Benedict uses this term repeatedly, defining *eros* as "that love between man and woman which is neither planned nor willed, but somehow imposes itself upon human beings" (paragraph 3). He recognizes the rich ambiguity of this force, that "somehow imposes itself" beyond a sure rational control, as the source of every creative and fruitful love.

Benedict acknowledges that *eros*, when "reduced to 'sex' becomes a commodity... to be bought and sold." But as *eros* is nurtured and purified, this human dynamic is "supremely ennobled," and "becomes able to attain its authentic grandeur" (paragraph 5). Benedict is bold enough to describe God's love for humans as *eros*. While God loves with the inclusive breadth of *agape*—embracing all humanity and playing no favorites—God also loves each person particularly and passionately, and this merits the name of *eros*. "God loves and his love may certainly be called *eros*, yet it is also totally *agape*." In the letter, Benedict reverses a long tradition that had defined God's love as necessarily "spiritual"—that is, detached and disinterested. The biblical prophets, he reminds us, spoke often of "God's passion for his people using boldly erotic images" (paragraph 9).

Philosopher Charles Taylor reinforces the call to reclaim *eros*: "We have to recover a sense of the link between erotic desire and the love of God, which lies deep in the Biblical traditions, whether Jewish or Christian, and find new ways of giving expression to this." He contends that what will be required is that we "explore again the profound interpenetration of *eros* and the spiritual life. This terribly fraught area in Western Christendom, where the sexual meets the spiritual, urgently awaits the discovery of new paths to God."

PATHWAYS OF EROS TODAY

The most familiar face of *eros* is sexual attraction and the affection this engenders. Reducing *eros* to sexuality and sexuality to sex is tempting, but the energy of *eros* moves us in many life-giving ways. *Eros* begets wonder and fascination with the sensual delights of creation, the endless ways in which the shapes and sounds and sights of the world move and enliven us.

For Anne Bathurst Gilson, "*Eros* connects a strong self-love, an opening to love of neighbors, and a love of God." This vital force "celebrates the sexual, the bodily, the earthly; it is rooted in body-experience and seeks the integration of body and spirit, human and divine."

Eros is most often associated with sexual arousal, but essayist Noelle Oxenhandler recognizes its presence in the midst of parenting. She describes the overwhelming delight of caring for her baby daughter. "I remember how palpably I experienced her too-muchness; it was a shudder in my body, an energy I had to soften, rein in, lest I squeeze her too hard, startle her with too exuberant a kiss." She adds, "It is this feeling I want to call the *eros* of parenthood: an upswelling of tenderness, often with a tinge of amazement."

Eros appears as well in the varied movements of desire and longing. *Eros* stirs in absence, in the pangs of solitude, in our lament for desires unfulfilled. *Eros* awakens us to suffering: we are aroused by our own pain and moved by the anguish of others. The erotic stirring of compassion moves us toward actions of solidarity and care.

The deep ambiguity of *eros*—its potential for both creativity and destruction—has long been recognized. And across history, human cultures and religious traditions have advocated ways to cultivate this volatile energy. The goal of this cultivation is that *eros* become not less passionate, but more personal; not less energetic, but more generous. It is not only our sexual passion but also the many faces of *eros* that await this cultivation.

With cultivation, *eros* expands from romantic attraction toward lifelong devotion, from a twinge of emotional pity toward courageous acts in pursuit of justice, from the early surges of empathy into the mature ability to recognize strangers, foreigners, and even enemies as "like us"—beloved children of God.

The charm of *eros* lies in its energy—the surge of delight, the arousal of passion, the stirring of compassion, the rush of pleasure. *Eros* is an ebullient, eager, and sometimes disruptive energy that moves us again and again toward more life. This reaching out may be filled with tenderness or driven by insatiable greed. But the energy of *eros* also opens pathways to our passionate God.

FOR FURTHER REFLECTION

The word *eros* may seem unfamiliar, but the experience of *eros* is not. Take a few moments now to acknowledge the movements of this dynamic energy in your own life:

> *Eros* as physical vigor
>
> *Eros* as longing or desire
>
> *Eros* as compassion
>
> *Eros* as sexual arousal
>
> *Eros* as love

Which of these faces of *eros* is most familiar to you? Recall a recent experience of this movement of *eros* in your life.

Which of these faces of *eros* is unfamiliar to you or distant from your own experience?

Beyond our brief list above, is there another movement of *eros* that is significant in your life now?

2

Naming Grace

RECEIVING GOD'S BLESSING AND FAVOR

Grace is a spiritual quality
of nourishment, of challenge, of healing
that is registered in our bodies

Grace dwells at the center of Christian life. "Amazing grace," celebrated in the familiar hymn, awakens us to faith and brings us back from every failure. But what is this mysterious reality? Over centuries, Christian understandings of grace have become increasingly abstract. *Eros* and grace seemed to inhabit very different worlds. Grace belongs to a spiritual realm and descends from heaven to heal and help us sinners. *Eros* belongs to the earthly realm, a physical domain of sexuality and passion. What do these two so different realities have to do with one another?

When we acknowledge the vital energy of *eros* as having its home in our Creator, and when we recognize that all grace flows from a generous God, we begin to sense the partnership of *eros* and grace.

- *Behold a graceful dancer. Her body moves in a fluid rhythm. We know that her leaps and turns must be long-rehearsed, but they seem free and spontaneous. This sensual movement stirs our hearts with delight as the dancer's body moves like a prayer.*

19

- *Behold a gracious host. As you enter his home, you initially feel ill at ease among so many other guests. The host quickly approaches you and welcomes you. He takes your coat, points out other friends in the room, and eases your discomfort.*

- *Behold a grateful heart. Surgery and months of chemotherapy have depleted a person's spirit and almost completely devastated her body. Days go by with little change until one morning she feels ever so slightly better. Hope stirs as she perceives this small but significant change and her heart fills with gratitude.*

Graceful, gracious, grateful—each springs from the word *grace*. Grace points to the surprising blessings that enliven the body and renew the spirit. In the Catholic heritage, grace identifies a spiritual quality—nourishment, healing, transformation—that is registered in our bodies. Grace lies beyond our expectations or merit, infusing life with a strength and vitality that we neither generate nor control.

As *eros* names the vital energy that stirs us to fullness of life, *grace* names God's powerful presence within and among us. The grace of *eros* flashes in the lively connections that link us to life, the many engagements through which our lives expand and become more graceful. The *eros* of grace fuels our fruitfulness, in children born of our love and in the diverse creations and contributions of our lives. Recognizing these gifts from our gracious God, we give thanks.

GRACE AS BLESSING (BARAKA)

Blessings mark the progress of creation in the Bible. At each stage—with the appearance of water, light, land and vegetation, animals—the Creator "saw that it was good." With the creation of human persons, "God blessed them, saying, 'Be fruitful and multiply'" (Gen 1:22). Since our earliest beginnings, God's blessings have called forth life in abundance.

In God's relationship with the chosen people, blessings continued, with promises of fertility and extravagant fullness of life. In Psalm 65, God's blessings include the plentiful rain and abundant crops of a year filled with bounty. The covenant binding this people to God exchanged obedience for abundant blessings: "If you will only obey the LORD your God . . . all these blessings shall come upon you and overtake you" (Deut 28:1–2).

The Israelites were blessed in their cities and in their fields, in their labor and in their children. God instructed Moses to pass on God's blessings though the words of the famous prayer of *baraka* (blessing): "You shall say to them, 'The Lord bless you and keep you; the Lord make his light to shine upon you and be gracious to you; the Lord lift up his countenance and give you peace" (Num 6:24). Blessing and grace were thus explicitly joined.

Scripture scholar Xavier Leon-Dufour defines God's blessings as expressions of God's lavish generosity. In Psalm 65, God's blessings "make life gush forth," and the blessings that the patriarchs spoke over their families called down "powers of fecundity and of life" on their sons.

We experience God's blessings in the many "coincidences in our favor." A married couple reflects on the seemingly chance events that led to their initial meeting; what "might not have been" initiated all the fruitfulness of their years together. Beholding their newborn child, even non-believing parents pronounce themselves "blessed."

As we feel blessed by God, so we are empowered to pronounce blessings. Praying a blessing as we are about to eat, we do not magically charge the food with divine power. But we acknowledge the ordinary meal as something more than ordinary; we acknowledge food as a gift that gives us pleasure while sustaining and renewing our lives. In such gestures, we enhance the significance of the everyday meal. Its nourishment now includes more than calories. With our prayers, we acknowledge the meal not only as food, but as gift.

We may also become aware of grace through experiencing a "brush with God." We use the expressions "a brush with the law" or "a brush with death" to suggest an approach by something significant, a perilous contact that comes too close for comfort. When Moses begged for greater intimacy with God, God issued a warning: "You cannot see my face, for no one shall see me and live" (Ex 33:20). Then God decided to compromise. God would place Moses in the cleft of a rock—between a rock and a hard place—and shield Moses' eyes as God brushed past. This mysterious story is about grace—about "finding favor"—and about how close we might come in intimacy with God.

Jacob had a close encounter with God in his night-time struggle with a mysterious stranger (Gen 32). Jacob had left his family and was facing the night alone. During this dark time, Jacob was attacked by an unknown assailant. As they wrestled, Jacob asked the attacker's name. No answer was given to Jacob, but he was required to reveal his own identity. As the harrowing struggle continued, Jacob was unable to defeat his opponent. But Jacob demanded a blessing and this was granted. In Jacob's sweaty "brush with God," *eros* and grace embraced.

Whether we identify ourselves as religious or not, we recognize similar encounters. In a sudden crisis or a chronic illness, in a failed relationship or a struggle with addiction, we have experienced our own "brush with God." The experience may wound us as it did Jacob. It may bring about new intimacy with God, as in Moses' case, or it may be more explicitly erotic, as with Ruth. We are surprised, confounded, or consoled by these encounters; here *eros* and grace unveil something of the mystery of God. The Christian journey is a lifelong process during which we become more open to such mysterious events. These "brushes with God" not only wound, but can also expand and heal our lives.

"FINDING FAVOR"—EROS AND GRACE

In the biblical book of Ruth, the experience of "finding favor" is erotic and sexual. When Ruth found favor with Boaz, Ruth lay with him on the threshing floor and "the Lord made her to conceive and bear a son." Her finding favor was the grace of a lifetime. But this phrase, "finding favor," appears throughout the Bible to name the many blessings that God mysteriously sends to make us more fully alive. When we find favor with God, *eros* and grace embrace.

- *Abraham and Sarah, already past childbearing age, learned that they would bear a son. This unlikely gift of sexual fruitfulness (eros as grace) prepared them for a significant vocation: Having found favor with God, they were chosen to generate a great nation. This gift was beyond anything they could have merited or anticipated, an exceptional act that revealed God's extravagance.*

- *The biblical writers remembered that long before Abraham there had been a catastrophic flood. But the deluge had not destroyed all of life. Among those saved from this devastation were Noah and his family, for Noah had "found favor" with the Lord.*

- *At another critical juncture in history, Moses learned in an intimate conversation with Yahweh that he had "found favor in God's sight" (Ex 33:12). But this was not enough for Moses; he implored the Lord, "If I have found favor in your sight, show me your ways so I may know you." Moses longed for an even closer relationship with his God, the favor found in seeing Yahweh face to face.*

Grace as blessing and grace as *finding favor* come together in the New Testament account of Mary's pregnancy. Surprised by the new life within her, Mary learns that she has found favor with God. In Luke's gospel Mary's cousin Elizabeth reveals the significance of this favor: "Blessed are you among women and blessed is the fruit of your womb" (Lk 1:42). Here, too, blessing is expressed in fertility and new life. Blessings and favors grace our lives and give us hope for life in abundance.

In his New Testament writings Paul used the Greek terms *charis* and *charisma* to express the Hebrew notion of "finding favor." *Charis* names the gift with which God favors us; this is grace as it flows from God. *Charisma* refers to the various abilities and talents with which God favors members of a faith community—gifts given to build up the body of believers. This is grace as it gives shape to our lives.

For Paul, *charis* is that gracefulness Christians recognize as a gift from a loving God. Spiritual gifts such as preaching, teaching, and discernment are *charisma* firmly anchored in our bodies. A gifted preacher uses her body—posture, eyes, voice, gestures—to deliver a message that awakens and strengthens our belief. A boring sermon or an uninspired lecture on doctrine is devoid of *eros*, and distances us from enlivening grace. The pleasing ability to sing, the robust gift of resolving conflicts, and the talent to deal with the complexities of administration—these too are spiritual charisms grounded in our bodies. The wide sweep of *charis* makes us graceful: poised in our bodies, adept in relationships, sensitive in compassion, and agile even in our brushes with God.

Paul's genius was to understand that grace is embodied in individuals and in the community of believers. Paul's writings have sometimes been interpreted to suggest a great divide between the flesh and the spirit, but when he writes about *charis*, he honors the intimacy of grace and *eros*.

Eros and Grace Embrace

During the decades when the New Testament texts were being crafted, a Roman writer reflected on the fruitfulness of *eros*. The first-century author Plutarch, who was not a Christian, composed his "Dialogue on Love" in the same language and within the same milieu as that of the New Testament authors. With an optimism that was unusual in his era, Plutarch traced the connections between *eros* and grace in married love. He writes:

> Physical pleasure with a spouse is the seed of friendship and the participation in great mysteries. Though the physical pleasure is brief, from it grows day by day respect and grace, affection and faithfulness.

Plutarch directly links pleasure and fruitfulness, using the same vocabulary we find in the Bible. Physical pleasure, though of brief duration, "causes to bloom" four special virtues of marriage. Plutarch evokes a horticultural image for the *eros* of sexual pleasure, which engenders not only children but also a richer, fuller love between the partners. Pleasure is intrinsic to the blooming of married love.

The four virtues Plutarch identifies as growing from such erotic pleasure—respect, grace, affection, and fidelity—are all mentioned in the New Testament. For the virtue of respect that grows between the couple, Plutarch uses the Greek word *time*; this same word appears in the New Testament with the meaning of respect, honor, or esteem. In 1 Peter 3, the word carries an erotic or at least matrimonial nuance as husbands are exhorted to respect their wives. In 1 Corinthians 12, Paul calls Christians to respect those most fragile, "inferior" parts of the body Christian. In Hebrews 13:4, the writer directs Christians to "hold marriage in honor."

For Plutarch, sexual pleasure also engenders the virtue of affection. *Agapesis* is the generous devotion expressed in the Latin *caritas*. In the Christian tradition, of course, *agape* came to represent the very antithesis of *eros*—the one a disinterested, spiritual care for others, the other a selfish grasping after erotic gratification. Plutarch dared to suggest that human *eros*—the powerful arousal that first attracts us to our life partner—matures over years of mutual commitment into the generous and devoted love of *agapo*.

Plutarch also found that faithfulness and trust followed the shared experience of sexual delight. In the New Testament, *pistis* usually denotes a believer's faith in God, but this fidelity is echoed in our enduring commitments to one another. The core marital virtue of fidelity grows out of a couple's shared love. The virtue of trust deepens as we come to know that we can rely on one another, and as we learn to surrender our defenses, once so necessary, to make possible a fuller embrace. Theologian Jim Cotter summarizes this special link of *eros* and fidelity by recalling "those finer vibrations of pleasure that come from the complete trust that two people have in each other when they are faithful over a long period of time."

If the virtues of respect, affection, and fidelity resonate with New Testament sentiments, the fourth virtue comes closest to the heart of the gospel. Plutarch believed that shared sexual pleasure engenders a certain kind of grace—a *charis*—in faithful lovers. The distinctive style of shared life that a couple develops over time together is rooted in shared erotic pleasure. Commenting on Plutarch's discussion, historian Peter Brown describes this grace of marriage as "the indefinable quality of mutual trust and affection gained through the pleasure of the bed." Plutarch employs the vocabulary of grace that stands at the core of the gospel. Christians experience the gracefulness of *charis* as the gift of a loving God. This is an embodied grace, for our charisms are manifested as visible, tangible actions that build up the body of Christ.

Charis harbors another, more explicitly erotic nuance. The verb *charizesthai* means "to gratify," to pleasure another in a way that evokes gratitude. In *The Symposium*, Plato used this verb to describe the gratifying of a lover's body (182a, 218c). Many Christian couples today share Plutarch's conviction that lovemaking can be a holy exercise in gratification. As we pleasure one another, we are not self-absorbed but thankful—to one another and to God, the source of all *charis*. In such love, *eros* and grace lie down together.

Graceful actions among Christians "gratify" the body of Christ. Three examples help rescue *gratification* from its more negative nuances.

- *When we take time to prepare a delicious meal to welcome a friend or celebrate a family anniversary, we gratify those we love. Those who share the delights of a lovingly prepared meal are pleasured and give thanks. Their gratification is at once sensual and spiritual.*

- *A liturgical dance gratifies the gathered body of the church. Such physical prayer pleases our eyes, raises our spirits, and makes us grateful. Some months ago, we participated in a multi-cultural Eucharist that concluded a national convention. At the offertory procession, young men and women in native Filipino dress gracefully brought the gifts forward. Swaying to a sensual rhythm these young worshipers added a scintillating dimension to this traditional ceremony.*

- *Caring for someone who is sick can also be an exercise in* charis. *As we wash a fevered body and change soiled bed linens for sheets that are fresh and clean, we gratify the body. Rubbing lotion on a stiff back evokes groans of gratitude; this, too, is a sensual grace.* Charis *is embodied grace in which flesh and spirit embrace. Gratitude is the evoked emotion that binds pleasure to fruitfulness.*

THE DIVORCE OF EROS AND GRACE

In the Hebrew Scriptures the sensual and the graceful moved comfortably together in the lives of the faithful. "Finding favor" was experienced in intimate arenas of life; grace found a dwelling-place in frail, appreciative bodies.

The seeds of separation—a disharmony that led to an ultimate divorce of *eros* and grace–were already present in the New Testament. Although Paul authorized an understanding of grace as embodied gifts, his language sometimes suggested a deep divide between the flesh and the spirit. "Those who live according to the flesh set their minds on the things of the flesh, but those who live according to the spirit set their minds on the things of the spirit" (Rom 8:5). By "flesh" Paul meant not our physical bodies but those habits, fleshly and otherwise, that are selfish or destructive. But over time many Christians missed this subtle distinction and envisioned a necessary antagonism between body and soul, flesh and spirit. Such dualism in the human heart would threaten any companionship of *eros* and grace.

Centuries later Christian theologians, eager to defend religious belief from the intrusions of modern science, built a firewall between faith and reason. The result was a vision of grace as part of a "supernatural" sphere that existed far above nature. This distance was meant to protect theological doctrine from the criticism of reason and science. As a consequence, supernatural realities were disengaged from everyday life. This divide reinforced the split between body and soul, between *eros* and grace.

Christians, it seemed, inhabited a two-storey world: above, the exalted domain of God, heaven and grace; below, the turmoil and passion of human life. In such a climate, spirituality was increasingly disengaged from worldly affairs: private prayer took priority over engagement in public life; an overwhelming concern for sexual purity crowded out commitments to social responsibility.

During the last half-century Christians have begun to recover ancient convictions about the intimacy of *eros* and grace. We are once again beginning to recognize that there is but one reality—a single creation given to us by God and, in the words of Karl Rahner, "permeated by the grace of God." Rahner continues: "The world is constantly and ceaselessly possessed by grace from its innermost roots." And, as theologian Michael Skelley reminds us, "the experience of God is primarily to be found hidden in the midst of ordinary life, in our experiences of hope, responsibility, love and death."

The "two-storey world" is no more. Instead we are reacquainting ourselves with this one world where we find favor with God. In this single reality we recognize the many faces of *eros* —in curiosity and creativity and affection; in imagination and suffering and hope—and we name grace in all the surprising ways it brings us to life in abundance.

FOR FURTHER REFLECTION

This chapter explores biblical images that ground the Christian understanding of grace.

Take one of the following images as the focus of prayerful reflection now:

> Grace as blessing, given and received
>
> Grace as finding favor with God
>
> Grace as charism, spiritual gifts registered in the body
>
> Grace as loving actions, gratifying the body of Christ

You might begin in a meditative mood, simply repeating the phrase that connects most directly with your experience of grace. Allow your mind to become quiet, empty of distractions and decisions. Then open your attention to the memories and feelings that emerge as you savor this mantra of grace. Bring your meditation to a close with a prayer of praise or thanksgiving.

3

Discovering Our God of Passion and Extravagance

*The prophets...described God's passion for God's people
using broadly erotic images.*
— Benedict XVI

To support the marriage of *eros* and grace—where the volatile life force that runs through creation meets the surprising healing power of God—we return to ancient biblical convictions. There we meet a God who is at once both vulnerable and extravagant. This mysterious Lord is the wellspring of both *eros* and grace.

Christians are pledged to a passionate God. In scripture we find not a disengaged deity overseeing our world from a distance but a gracious power alive to both prophets and mystics. The Bible reveals God as *Shekinah* (faithful presence), as *Ruah* (animating spirit), and as *Emmanuel* (God-with-us). In story after story, the Hebrew Scriptures record a God who is profoundly engaged with humanity—moved by our suffering, dismayed by our folly, angered by our injustices, zealous for our well-being, and always, persistently, moving toward us in love.

The New Testament, too, reveals God as passionately involved with humanity. Jesus names this mysterious power *Abba*, loving Father. In compassion, the Father sends the Son into the world, not to condemn but to redeem, to hasten humanity's return to the heart of the Divine Mystery. The Spirit, poured out from the heart of God, continues this vital embrace of all creation, across the cosmos and throughout human history.

MEETING A PASSIONATE GOD

In the book of Exodus, we are introduced to "a God merciful and gracious, slow to anger and abounding in steadfast love and faithfulness" (Ex 34). In Psalm 103, we again meet a God who is "merciful and gracious, slow to anger, and abounding in compassion." In the prophet Hosea (11:8–9), this tension between the passions of anger and care finds a more powerful expression as "My heart recoils within me; my compassion grows warm and tender, I will not execute my fierce anger." Jewish scholar Abraham Heschel dared to name this alternation of anger and compassion as the "mood swings" in the heart of God.

Christians at first might pale at the thought of divine mood swings, but we are slowly returning to biblical portraits of God moved by powerful passions. The story of the flood and Noah's life-saving action (Gen 6:6) begins with the observation that "the Lord was sorry that he had made humankind on the earth and it grieved him to his heart." Joshua writes of a God who is jealous (Josh 24:19). Are these accounts of regret, compassion, jealousy, and grief merely "primitive tales" that mistakenly attribute human feelings to a transcendent deity? Or do they reveal essential characteristics of the mystery we call God?

Early in our tradition, the defenders of Christian faith faced challenging questions from intellectuals in the Roman Empire. The death of Jesus, the beloved Son of God, seemed to them an insurmountable scandal. How could divinity enter human life and then suffer such a humiliating, disastrous end? According to the prevailing philosophy at that time, a transcendent deity must be beyond all change, show no vulnerability, and exist on an exalted plane, untouched by the passions that constantly unsettle the hearts of fragile mortals.

The early Christian apologists rose to the challenge by refashioning the biblical God—a God of passion, desire, and *eros*—into the equal of any philosophical deity. Theologians in the West began to describe God as perfect substance. Such a transcendent substance would necessarily be self-sufficient; it could have no intrinsic relation with creation (since this would limit God's perfection) and would be subject to no desire or passion. If this description satisfied philosophers, it diverged sharply from biblical memories. Scripture showed God deeply engaged in covenant relationships, mutual commitments that led to expressions of anger and compassion. In the eleventh century, Anselm agonized over this non-biblical image when he prayed, "How are you compassionate and at the same time passionless? For if you are passionless, you do not feel sympathy; if you do not feel sympathy, your heart is not wretched from sympathy with the wretched, but this is to be compassionate."

The Greek-speaking church of Eastern Christianity, more comfortable with a God of passion, found no difficulty in speaking of God and *eros* in the same context. But the understanding of God as autonomous, self-sufficient, and beyond all desire and passion would prevail in Western theology. So Augustine would write: "God himself, according to the scriptures, becomes angry and yet is never disturbed by any passions whatsoever." A dispassionate God was divorced from any association with *eros*.

In the course of the twentieth century, Catholic scholars in Europe began the long pilgrimage back to the Bible. They looked again at the revelation given in many enigmatic stories and compelling images of scripture. From this painstaking research began to emerge the picture of a passionate, even erotic God. In the Hebrew Scriptures we have seen the many emotions that filled God's heart. Our reflection on the New Testament will reveal a surprisingly human Jesus.

REMEMBERING JESUS' PASSIONS

Many Christians grew up with the description of Jesus as "meek and humble of heart." They were taught that, because he is the

Son of God, Jesus stands above the disturbing movements of passion that mark our own lives. But the gospels tell a different story—of a Jesus who is like us in all things except sin.

One of the most gripping expressions of passion in Jesus' life is reported in Matthew's gospel. Near the end of his life, Jesus sat on a hill overlooking Jerusalem, grieving, "How often have I desired to gather your children together as a hen gathers her brood under her wings, and you were not willing" (Mt 23:37).

The passion of anger, often identified as one of the seven deadly sins, erupted frequently in Jesus' life. He became enraged over moneychangers who were operating at the entrance to the temple (Mt 21:12–13). He was angered by those who baited him over the niceties of Jewish sabbath law (Mk 3:5). He showed his fury at hypocrites, whom he compared to "whitened sepulchers" (Mt 23:27).

John's gospel uses a single Greek word to express the distress that pulled at Jesus' heart in the last months of his life. When Jesus learned that his friend Lazarus had died, he became "greatly disturbed" (Jn 11:38). Later, as he faced his death, Jesus said, "Now my soul is troubled" (Jn 12:27), and when he learned that Judas would betray him, we are told that "Jesus was troubled in spirit" (Jn 13:21). Yet in the next chapter of John, we read that Jesus urged his friends, "Do not let your hearts be troubled" (Jn 14:27). Of course, their hearts *were* troubled, just as Jesus' heart was repeatedly distressed.

In these gospel accounts of Jesus' distress, we learn that passions are necessary disturbances. Emotions ground us in our world, so we must expect to be moved by what is happening around us. Faced with a significant loss, we necessarily experience grief. Meeting an attractive person, we are understandably stirred with delight. If the world around us is depressing, we ourselves ought to feel depressed. Christian spirituality is not about avoiding our emotions in the hope of sustaining a stoical, dispassionate existence. Instead, our spiritual quest is to attune our surges of anger, grief, and delight to the movements of passion that we see in the life of Jesus.

OUR GOD OF EXTRAVAGANCE

In the biblical portrait we find a Lord of extravagance as well as a God of passion. In creation itself and in God's prodigal love for humankind we see evidence of an affection that knows no bounds. But in contemporary America, many Christians may be put off by negative connotations of extravagance. Here, where the economy depends on conspicuous consumption and the gap between rich and poor continues to grow, extravagance signals vice more often than virtue. Nevertheless, recalling divine extravagance gives significant insight into the heart of God.

God's extravagance is on display throughout creation. We inhabit a universe that dazzles with its size and diversity. Astronomers inform us of the unthinkable enormity of multiple galaxies and innumerable black holes. The long-time director of the Vatican observatory notes that there are 10^{22} stars in the universe (this abbreviation signals the number 10 followed by twenty-two zeroes). There is more helium in the universe than all the stars could have produced; this superabundance can be explained only by some "big bang" explosion, an event that took place in the earliest stages of a very hot cosmos. We learn that the universe and our planet existed for billions of years before humans came on the scene. These outsized numbers stretch the limits of our comprehension.

And biologists tell us of the myriad species that populate this world; for example, fourteen hundred species of ants have been identified. How to explain this abundance? The extraordinary shapes and colors of the tropical fish swimming in an aquarium astonish and delight us. Then there is the annual profusion of acorns dropped by a single oak tree every autumn. The lavishness of creation staggers the imagination. A boundless generosity is constantly on exhibit throughout our world.

The question arises: What is the meaning of this excess? Why this overwhelming immensity and complexity, this "muchness"? Could extravagance itself be a signature of God's creation? The Greek-speaking theologian Gregory of Nyssa, writing in the fourth century, asserted that the word "*eros* translates better than *agape* the excess of love the soul can have when its eyes are fixed upon the inaccessible beauty of the divine nature."

The Bible is a record of God's extravagant affection for humanity, an affection given constant expression in God's gracious actions toward us. An early hint of the extent of God's affection appears in the covenant with Israel. Initially God laid down explicit conditions for this agreement: If people would obey God's laws, a lasting covenant would bind them to God. Then, they would be God's people and he would be their God (for example, see Jer 7:23 and 11:4; Ezek 11:20 and 14:11; Hos 2:23).

In time, God seems to have abandoned this conditional arrangement (perhaps because it was so regularly violated?) and offered a covenant written not on stone, but in each person's heart (Jer 31:33). This covenant was to be rooted not in Israel's righteous observance, but in God's unaccountable extravagance. In our own time, as we saw above, Benedict XVI reclaims *eros* as a fitting description of God's unbounded love for us.

Philosopher Paul Ricoeur encourages a reflection that brings us more deeply into an appreciation of God's extravagance. He points to two different but complementary dynamics in God's mysterious presence among us. Biblical accounts often announce "a logic of equivalence," revealed in God's demands for justice. But the Bible also celebrates "a logic of superabundance," revealed in God's extravagance.

The God of justice may be more familiar. Even those who no longer embrace the biblical God can readily recall the Bible's apparent call to retribution: "an eye for an eye, a tooth for a tooth" (Ex 21:24). This moral stance has strong appeal: We long for a universe that is moral, where justice requires that people get what they deserve. Jesus later rejected this harsh approach to justice, but many of us still cling to an ideal of avenging every wrong.

We meet the logic of equivalence again in the memorable statement, "You reap whatever you sow" (Gal 6:7). In his second letter to the Corinthians Paul comments, "The one who sows sparingly will also reap sparingly and the one who sows bountifully will also reap bountifully" (2 Cor 9:6). These biblical passages have given rise to a spirituality based on a righteous God who measures our virtues and vices, preparing to reward us according to our due. From this image grows a piety of caution and even calculation. Have I done enough? Do my good deeds outweigh my bad deeds? Have I earned my salvation yet?

A century before Paul, the Roman writer Cicero made a similar observation: "If you do not work, you do not eat." This idea has great appeal as folk wisdom. It seems only fair that people should be rewarded in proportion to the work they have put into a project. What could be more just? In a moral universe, we would be repaid in direct proportion to our investment.

Despite the appeal of such a view, life teaches us that things do not always work out this way—and sometimes it is to our benefit. Often we reap what another has sown. We inherit unearned resources and unmerited goods from the efforts of an earlier generation. We plant our hopes and values in the generation to come, yet do not ourselves live long enough to see the fruit of this "sowing." So the notion of equivalence, however familiar and comforting, is as often false as it is true.

The moral ideal of balance and equality continues in the New Testament when Jesus urges his followers, "Love one another as I have loved you" (Jn 15:12). In the moral imperative given as the great commandment, Jesus announces, "You shall love the Lord your God with all your heart, and with all your soul, and with all your mind. This is the greatest and first commandment. And a second is like it: you shall love your neighbor as yourself" (Mt 22:37–39). We must love God above all else, and then we are to balance our self-care with care for others. This is an ideal of equality and balance, the world of *logos*—good order, harmony, and justice, and the equal expression of love.

BIBLICAL EXTRAVAGANCE

The second dynamic that runs through the Bible, complementing the call to equality and justice, is "a logic of superabundance," which points to a God known for extravagance. We saw a hint of this in the changing conditions of the covenant: Instead of a series of mandates establishing a well-balanced relationship between humans and their Creator, a sacred *quid pro quo*, God now opts for a covenant without conditions. Such an arrangement suggests another world order, one in which love wells up beyond all measure. This is the world not of *logos* but of *eros*.

In Matthew's gospel, Jesus meets the issue head-on: "You have heard it said, 'an eye for an eye, a tooth for a tooth,' but I say to you, do not resist an evildoer. But if anyone strikes you on the right cheek, turn the other also" (Mt 5:38–39). Vengeance and a thirst for strict justice are being replaced by something else, a new law that is both surprising and extravagant.

Elsewhere Jesus shares with the disciples his vision of giving and receiving. "Give and it will be given to you." At first, this seems to reinforce the logic of equivalence. But Jesus adds "A good measure, pressed down, shaken together, running over, will be put in your lap" (Lk 6:38). Generosity will be repaid not with an equal portion but with excess, "running over." This gospel statement calls to mind a ritual celebrated in many cultures: Wine is poured into a small ceremonial cup until it overflows—not in error, but with intent. An observer—especially a Western observer—might well rush forward, urging the pourer to stop, saying, "Don't waste the wine! You will stain the table." But the very point of the ceremony is to demonstrate excess and extravagance. Such rituals celebrate blessings that overflow the small cups of our lives. Linking these two images, we might say that our God is a Creator who does not know when to stop pouring.

The gospels overflow with parables of extravagance and excess. A tiny seed sprouts into a gigantic tree, a few seeds scattered on good ground multiply, not twofold or tenfold, but a hundredfold (Mk 4:8).

A wayward son, having wasted his inheritance, is welcomed home by his father in a display of extravagant affection. Workers who are hired in the final hour of the day receive a full day's wages. This generosity evokes grumbling from those who have worked the entire day: "These last have worked only one hour and you have made them equal to us who have borne the burden of the day and the scorching heat" (Mt 20:12). But the master replies to those who are looking for just treatment, "Are you envious because I am generous?"

In all of these parables, the revelation is not about doing things properly or in good measure, but about an excessively generous response. Ricoeur describes such parables as employing a "rhetoric of excess" to point to God's extravagance. The message seems to be that we do not receive what we deserve (thanks be to God!). Instead, we are loved excessively by our God and receive blessings we neither merit nor can account for.

Jesus' parables of extravagance are echoed by Paul's vocabulary of excess. Paul uses a single Greek word (*perisseuein*) twenty-two times to express God's extravagance. In his letter to the Ephesians, he writes of "the riches of his grace that God has *lavished* on us" (Eph 1:8). To the Philippians he offers, "This is my prayer, that your love may *overflow*" (Phil 1:9). In 1 Thessalonians, he prays, "May the Lord make you increase and *abound* in love for one another" (1 Thess 3:12). Lavish...overflow...abound—these are all efforts to translate the Greek word that Paul repeatedly uses to express God's extravagant grace. Theologian David Ford describes these passages as examples of Paul's "rhetoric of abundance...the pervasive sense of a lavish generosity in blessing, loving, revealing, and reconciling."

SCARCITY AND ABUNDANCE

In the Gospel of John, the Jesus we meet is not confined to well-balanced actions. Instead, he feeds large crowds and forgives abundantly. Here Jesus announces his mission: "I have come so they may have life, and have it in abundance" (Jn 10:10). The goal is not survival, but flourishing; not simple existence but life in abundance. Paul picks up this theme in his letter to the community in Rome, when he proclaims that through the life and death of Jesus, "when sin increased, grace abounded all the more" (Rom 5:20).

The core account of Jesus' commitment to abundance—the feeding the multitude—appears five times in the synoptic gospels—the story itself multiplied, perhaps, to emphasize its importance. (Mt 14, Mark 6, and Luke 9 all tell the same version of the story, and Matt 15 and Mark 8 retell it with somewhat different statistics.) A large crowd has come to listen to Jesus. Now the day is late and they are in a deserted spot—a scarcity of both time and resources. When Jesus tells his friends to feed the people, they complain that they have only a few loaves of bread and some fish. But when Jesus has blessed these resources and the food is distributed, there is—amazingly—more than enough to feed the entire group. "All ate and were filled. What was left over was gathered up, twelve baskets of broken pieces" (Lk 9:17).

The dialectic in this story is scarcity and abundance: an abundance of people satisfied through a scarcity of resources. Was this a one-time event, a miracle that only Jesus, the Son of God, could accomplish? Or is there, perhaps, a larger message here? Perhaps the story tells us that resources held in private and kept out of circulation generate a scarcity. When shared, these resources go further than we might have predicted; in fact, they become abundant. Apparent scarcity often obscures a hidden abundance.

THE HOLY SPIRIT—GOD'S LAVISH AMBASSADOR

When Christians emphasize the Creator God as a transcendent source of life and Christ as the Logos or Word of God, there seems little need for the shadowy "third person of the trinity," the Holy Spirit. In Western Christianity, Father and Son have filled the screen of our religious imagination. Over centuries, theologies of Christ have multiplied as discussions of the Spirit have all but disappeared.

During recent decades, as scholars have returned to the scriptural images of God, the Spirit has come back into focus. The

Spirit names a mysterious energy that surges surprisingly throughout the world. At Pentecost the first disciples were gathered in an upper room, pained by the absence of Jesus and engulfed in their own season of scarcity. Then the Spirit, experienced as both fire and wind, warmed their hearts and aroused them with new confidence. So we pray at Pentecost: "Send forth your Spirit and we will be recreated and you will renew the face of the earth."

God as Spirit enlivens and heals, as a wind that blows where it will. Paul describes this Spirit standing with us in times of distress, ready "to intercede with sighs too deep for words" (Rom 8:26). Bodily sighs, even beyond words, sometimes signal the Spirit's presence. In his letter to the Christians in Rome, Paul writes of "the whole creation groaning" as humanity yearns for liberation. Our hope, he reminds us, is not in our righteousness but in God's abounding grace. The Spirit—animating, arousing, healing—is a face of *eros* and the ambassador of God's extravagance.

FOR FURTHER REFLECTION

The Bible is rich with stories and images that celebrate the passion of God. Let this resource now be the focus of your prayerful reflection.

Return to the stories of the Hebrew Scriptures, recalling a passage that captures for you the powerful emotions in the heart of God—anger or affection, compassion or regret. Take time to explore this biblical account—prayerfully reading the text, identifying the passion at play, finding links to your own experience.

Then turn to the gospel texts, recalling one of the many stories of Jesus moved by strong emotion. Enter into the story, becoming present to the setting and circumstances, experiencing the passion of Jesus' response. Consider the ways in which your own passions—of desire, of sorrow, of hope—connect you with this passionate Jesus.

Now, turn to celebrate your experience of God's extravagance. Reflect on the words of Jesus: "Give and it will be given to you. A good measure, pressed down, shaken together, running over, will be put in your lap." Recall the ways in which this lavish generosity has been part of your own experience of God. Acknowledge the ways in which God's extravagance shapes your own generosity.

4

A Spirituality of Eros

PRAYING FOR OUR HEART'S DESIRE

Pray for what you desire.
— Ignatius of Loyola

Eros is the vital energy that moves us toward others, guiding our hopes for meaningful connections and a more fruitful life. *Eros* finds expression in our deepest desires, in our holy longings, and in our best hopes for abundant life.

In the *Spiritual Exercises*, Ignatius Loyola counsels those on the spiritual journey to "pray for what you desire." This advice, at the heart of Ignatian spirituality, reflects an extraordinary Catholic optimism—the belief that God's will for us can be discerned within our own deepest desires. If we can uncover and then trust our authentic longings, these will move us toward more generous lives.

Many centuries after Ignatius, the contemporary writer Ronald Rolheiser sounds the same optimism: "Spirituality concerns what we do with desire. It takes its root in the eros inside of us and it is all about how we shape and discipline this eros. Spirituality, essentially defined, is how we handle this eros." The spiritual journey invites us to pray for and discern the desires that would lead us to life in abundance.

The Wings of Desire

Our desires are notoriously difficult to name and to trust. We find in our hearts a bewildering array of dreams and hopes, fears and longings. Some desires seduce us, while others have the capacity to lead us toward greatness.

Psychiatrist Mark Epstein describes the baffling range of desires that occupy our hearts: "We feel incomplete and desire completeness; we feel unrest and desire ease; we feel insecurity and desire comfort; we feel alone and desire connection." As we harbor all these feelings, we often find ourselves caught between the conflicting movements of anxiety and desire. Both these energies face us toward the future, but desire opens us to the unknown while anxiety counsels a retreat.

These two internal dynamics lead in different directions: desire moves us out of ourselves toward the possibility of relationship, while anxiety holds back in the safety of a self that is already known. For Epstein, "desire is our vitality." The *eros* of desire "is the crucible within which the self is formed." In this crucible, our personal hopes are often entangled in our family's plans for us and in our culture's norms and ideals. Our life becomes fruitful as we learn to sort out these multiple influences, trusting our deepest desires even in the face of social pressures that would point us in other directions.

How are we to unravel our best hopes from the needs and wants that entrap us? Recognizing different levels of need can be place to start. Water, food, and shelter head the list of basic needs without which we cannot survive. When we consider not just surviving but thriving, our needs expand to include language, love, community, and the opportunity for productive work and participation in our social and political world.

Michael Ignatieff adds to these needs a third level: "We have needs of the spirit because we are the only species whose fate is not simply a fact of our existence but a problem whose meaning we attempt to understand." If these needs—to find meaning in life and make sense of suffering and death—are less tangible, they are no less urgent.

Today these needs of the spirit may rank last among the supposed needs generated by advertising. Coaxed by commerce and commercials, we may become convinced that we "need" a pill to help us sleep, a jolt of caffeine in the late afternoon to supply extra energy, and yet another drug to boost our sexual performance. In a consumer culture, such endless needs are crucial to the ever-expanding economy to which our well-being has been fused.

Here, "needs" begin to overlap with an ever-expanding list of "wants." We may come, quite easily, to want the many items presented as "must buy" products or "must see" entertainment. Essential and legitimate human needs begin to mushroom and merge with wants, which themselves have multiplied again and again. In such a climate, how do we find our way to our deepest desires?

Our most authentic desires are situated well beyond the basic biological needs of food and shelter, and far beneath the surface "wants" that fuel a consumer society. Such desires—those that Ignatius encourages us to pray for—might involve finding a loving life companion, welcoming a child into the world, or choosing a career that is worthy of our life's efforts. These deep desires abide in the realm of *eros*, where our lives flourish.

Our most authentic desires emerge and endure in ways that console us. As we give ourselves more deeply in commitments of love or work, we recognize: "This is what I truly desire. Whatever the obstacles, this is my most compelling ambition." The accompanying mood of consolation assures us that this desire leads toward the abundant life that Jesus promises.

TRUSTING OUR DESIRES

Still, we wonder: Are our desires not dangerous? Many Christians find themselves distrustful of desires and instincts. Early in our heritage, desire became enmeshed with lust and selfishness. Influenced by a dualistic view of flesh and spirit, Christian writers often identified "the spirit" with the part of our humanity that wills only the good, while "the flesh" signified the bodily, passionate part that is driven by desires. If human desire is rooted in "the flesh," it seems guaranteed to lead us away from God. Reformation theology emphasized sinful human nature as inhabiting a "fallen" world. God's will and human desire seemed to have little to do with one another.

In the Garden of Eden, the original couple "saw that the tree was good for food, and that it was a delight to the eyes, and that the tree was to be desired" (Gen 3:6). The Bible's first mention of desire recalls a fateful choice that had catastrophic consequences. Our ancestors' earliest desire—as a temptation that they succumbed to—unraveled God's plans for paradise. This provides an inauspicious beginning to Christian reflection on desire.

In the New Testament, desire is often associated with lust or concupiscence. Recall the famous warning in Matthew's gospel that "anyone who looks at a woman *with lust* has already committed adultery with her in his heart" (Mt 5:28). Paul employs the same Greek word for desire when writing of the command, "You shall not *covet*" (Rom 7:7).

The association of desire with sinful passion reaches its extreme in the New Testament letter of St. James. Here, desire gone astray is personified as a female temptress who seduces a man, leading him to sin, and through his sin to death: "A person is tempted by his own desire, being lured and enticed by it; then when that desire has conceived, it gives birth to sin, and that sin, when it is fully grown, gives birth to death" (Jas 1:14–15). Now human desire is embedded in a sexual metaphor of female seduction that conjoins sexuality, sin, and death.

Desire's poor reputation continued among Christian scholars. At the end of the second century, Clement insisted that a true Christian "aims to have no desire at all." It was not a great leap for Augustine, two centuries later, to associate erotic desire with carnal lust, to define marriage as "a remedy for concupiscence," and finally, to link original sin with sexual intercourse. At that early moment in our tradition, desire's sinful reputation was firmly established. Little recognition of holy desires and their vital role in our everyday lives was offered to counterbalance this increasingly negative view.

Desire's bad reputation was again compounded in the sixteenth century. Despite the many positive reforms wrought by the Council of Trent (1545–1563), a new note of legalism was introduced into Catholic spirituality. Aquinas's question, "What must we do to be happy?" was replaced by "What does the law allow?" As this more legalistic approach gained acceptance, duty began to displace desire at the heart of Christian life. Sundays and feast days, previously understood as occasions for communal worship and celebration, were now designated as "days of obligation." A new emphasis on private confession gave heightened attention to duties neglected and a preoccupation with illicit sexual longing.

These developments deepened the distrust of desire as believers were counseled to look more often to authorities for guidance. Obedience to church mandates came to outweigh creativity or risk. Personal conscience, intended to aid in the discernment of desires, had little place in such a spirituality. The *eros* of religious passion drained from the lives of many Christians, to be replaced by docile obedience and chronic anxiety regarding sexuality.

REDEEMING OUR DESIRES

Theologian James Nelson reminds us that "the problem is not to uproot or transcend desire (which is an essential mark of our humanity and of our belonging to God), but rather to order all objects of our desire in accord with their true relation to God, in whom alone our restless hearts will find satisfaction and fulfillment." A signature of authentic desire is its ability to take us beyond ourselves, rescuing us from self-absorption and leading us into enlivening and generative relationships. If holy *eros* ignites our deepest desires, this grace leads us into commitments of love and service. Desire itself is a dynamic at the core of self-transcendence, a dynamic that moves us beyond our well-protected ego to engage with others in expressions of love, compassion, and generosity.

Our Jewish ancestors were not afraid of their passions or bodily urges; they turned their erotic longings into prayer: "My body aches for you like a dry and weary land" (Ps 63:1; authors' translation). In Psalm 37, we find a further link between God and our deepest desires: "Take delight in the LORD and God will give you the desires of your heart." These prayers encourage us to recover the deeply human desires that can energize and direct our journey toward God.

Following these biblical invitations, Christians dare to connect God's desires with their own. God's hopes and ambitions for our lives lie half-hidden in the desires that stir our hearts. In the inevitable ambiguities of our search, we can trust that God's desires in us do not conflict with the best interests of our deepest and truest selves. Joseph Tetlow, a leading authority on Ignatian spirituality, reinforces this intimate link between our desires and God's ambitions for us: "God our Creator and Lord writes his hopes into our desiring. If our hearts are made for Him, then He has planted deep, deep desires for Himself in our hearts."

A subtle shift is taking place today in Christian spirituality. Talk of *God's will* is gradually being replaced by discussion of *God's desire*. As we recover the biblical portrait of God as a mysterious presence alive with passion, we become comfortable reflecting on God's ambitions for us. An earlier piety had imagined a blueprint approach in which God wills, from all eternity, the specific choices we should make in our lives. In this scenario, we anxiously search for clues about what this micro-managing God has decided. Paralysis easily ensues as we fret about making a life choice that might depart from this already finished design.

Abandoning this model of God's will, Christian spirituality today recognizes a loving God who opens possibilities for a fruitful and generous life, and grants us the freedom and wherewithal (conscience and companions, wit and virtues) to craft our personal vocation. At the end of Ron Hansen's novel *Mariette in Ecstasy*, a devout woman appeals to God to show her how to proceed in her life. She has always, Mariette reminds God, sought to know and follow God's will. Now she prays again for guidance. And a deeper revelation emerges as she reflects on God's response: "We try to be formed and held and kept by him, but instead he offers us freedom. And now when I try to know his will, his kindness floods me, his great love overwhelms me, and I hear God whisper, 'surprise me.'" Might we not expect that after decades of forming a trust-worthy conscience, God would invite us to trust and follow our desires, those holy longings that have their origin in God's great ambitions for us?

Even with this more generous picture of God's engagement with us, we may wonder if we can really trust our desires. Spiritual writer Philip Sheldrake answers that "we can if we befriend them and then test them rather than try to ignore them or bypass them. Only by befriending and testing them can we gradually learn how to distinguish deep desire from wants." Befriending and testing our desires is a central dynamic of any life in the spirit. As wishes, wants, and desires surface, we must take the time to listen to them. Where do they come from? What do they reveal about our best hopes? Befriending our desire is an unending discipline of authentic Christian life.

Unrequited Desires and Restless Hearts

Eros, driven by desire, must learn to live with absence: a lover not yet returned; a life ambition that remains just out of reach. Absence instructs us in passionate detachment. *Eros* itself will often remain restless, as Augustine reminds us: "Our hearts are restless until they rest in You."

If restless desires are all that we know, our lives will not thrive. How are we to tolerate the gap between our longings and their realization? In fact, some longed-for goals will not be realized. A couple yearns to have a child, yet after much effort this hope remains unfulfilled. Someone else delights in the promise of a relationship ready to flower into committed love, only to see this hope defeated. A talented young person longs to become a concert pianist but gradually recognizes that her ability falls short of the demands of this profession. In such painful realizations, we sense that life's promise has been broken. Even God has let us down, as our deepest hope seems lost.

In such crises, two responses must be honored. First, the right to be angry, even with God. The psalmist has taught us that our anger can become prayer, connecting us with God in an expression of our grief. In time, with our anger spent, a second response becomes possible: We open our hearts to listen once more to this deep desire. Our earlier dream defeated, how may its deeper energy be recaptured? How else may our erotic longing—to foster new life, to connect deeply with another, to bring more beauty to the world—be satisfied? Gradually desire reawakens, urging our recommitment to life. If we remain alienated from this erotic energy, we will not thrive. So we open ourselves once again to our heart's desire.

Wendy Farley believes that "desire, as eros, is this God-given energy that lies beneath all our suffering. If we can connect with this deep energy, desire will guide us past and through all our mistakes, pain, losses, and moments of despair."

LIVING MORE DEEPLY INTO OUR DESIRES

Our acquisitive society and its invasive consumerism threaten to lure us into a permanent state of restlessness. Much in contemporary culture works against our finding contentment in our work, our relationships, or even in a leisurely meal shared with friends. Busy schedules leave little room for savoring such simple satisfactions. We dare not allow ourselves to rest in the midst of our unfinished lives. But if we are constantly diverted by conflicting wants and needs, our lives become a parody of Augustine's prayer. Our hearts are restless, but their dissipation does not echo God's desire.

Communities of faith, as gatherings of mature believers, help shape our restlessness toward more authentic desires. Through shared worship and common prayer and spiritual companionship and social action, many faith communities provide a place for the discernment of desires. And these communities are themselves enlivened by *eros*, the vital energy that opens us to the needs of the world.

FOR FURTHER REFLECTION

On a sheet of paper, draw a line that represents your life. This may be a simple straight line, or perhaps a spiral, or a more ambitious design with peaks and valleys to capture some of your life's changes. But prepare this basic sketch quickly, without any concern for artistic quality.

Then, along that line drawing place a mark—probably more than one—to identify a time in your life's journey when you followed your desire, perhaps by choosing or changing a career, or by deepening a relationship, or by embracing a new dream.

Now, with this life-line of desire before you, focus on a time when your desire proved trustworthy. Spend some moments letting this experience of desire become full again in your memory. Then turn to these questions:

> In this experience of desire, what impelled you forward?
>
> Why/how were you able to follow this desire?
>
> What obstacles did you experience? Where you tempted to hesitate or to turn away from this desire?
>
> What evidence in your life confirms that this was a trustworthy desire?
>
> From this experience of trustworthy desire, what encouragement or caution would you offer to others?

PART TWO

THE BODY'S ROMANCE WITH EROS

*A spirituality of eros is especially concerned with the body,
"temple of the Holy Spirit."*

*Christians believe—on our more hopeful days—
that grace is a spiritual gift registered in our bodies.*

*We can come to trust the body's wisdom, the information and insights
harbored in our nerves and muscles.*

*Eros matures in our sensuality
as our body attunes us to the glories and dangers of our world.*

*Rhythms of bodily energy support our mood of calm concentration
while overwork and anxiety can compromise this calm,
leaving us "tired and wired."*

*We reflect on our "body image"
often ruled by an unholy tyranny.*

*The body has great symbolic power,
as ornamental, instrumental, and sacramental.*

*And pleasure can make us more richly present to our lives or
distract us from pain and sorrow that we need to face.*

5

Eros in Everyday Life

SENSUALITY, EMOTION, SEXUALITY

You do not have to be afraid of emotions
for Eros is the true healer.
You only need to cultivate the passions that bind you to others
and to the living world.

— Carl Jung

ros is a source of life-giving connections. For ancient writers, *eros* named the energy that draws us toward the good, the true, and the beautiful. By contrast, the closest that contemporary usage comes to *eros* is the word *erotic*—a word with vaguely pornographic connotations, calling up images of illicit liaisons or perverse sexual practices. Psychologists and theologians today are restoring *eros*'s battered reputation. By drawing on the word's earliest meanings, they are reclaiming *eros* as the fundamental vitality of the human person. This broader meaning encompasses sexual arousal and more. *Eros* is ardent desire. Rooted in our bodies, *eros* links us passionately to life. *Eros* moves in all our efforts to make contact, to be—quite literally—in touch. Desire and delight, gratitude and compassion are gifts of *eros*, connecting us with other people in life-giving ways.

In human life, *eros* makes its debut early—in the uncomplicated delight of babies as they explore their bodies and their world. *Eros* is at play in the aura of contentment that surrounds a well-nurtured child. The infant nursing serenely at her mother's breast or held lovingly in his father's arms—this scene moves even the world-weary among us. And we pray the mystic's mantra—all will be well, all will be well, all manner of things shall be well.

Eros fuels the natural exuberance that healthy children display. Directing this energy is one of the tasks of growing up, but the maturing process can also put *eros* at risk. Many of us reach adulthood with our exuberance not only tamed but domesticated. Our well-socialized selves distrust spontaneity. Our stance toward life is responsible, resigned, or resentful, but enthusiasm is rare. We feel stuck, embedded in duties yet somehow disconnected from life. *Eros* seems to have retreated, taking with it vitality and joy.

The essential energy of *eros*, however, survives even our adult inhibitions. We tap into its power as our sensuality, our emotions, and our sexuality open us to the world and echo God's creative power.

CELEBRATING OUR SENSES

The body gives gifts to the spirit. The lazy contentment of a summer day, a brisk walk along the seashore, the warmth of a loving embrace, the pleasures of a meal shared with friends—these are benefits of our embodiment. Our bodies are stirred by beauty and moved by joy. And our bodies long to be touched—held in affection, caressed by a lover, soothed by a comforting hand. These gifts come to us through our senses, connecting us with the world and opening us to its delights.

Our eyes delight in color—in a fully blooming flower garden, in the splendor of a fall-hued hillside, in the majesty of a sunset. Color grabs our attention; it influences our appetite for food and our fashion choices. In some of us, the visual sense matures into a sophisticated awareness of shade, shape, and form, in appreciation of fine art or a talent for home decorating. What we see can arouse us or give rise to deep calm. The beauty of nature brings a sense of renewal in the solitude of a starry winter night, the majesty of a mountain view, the power of a waterfall.

Sound, too, comes as gift. Our hearts leap up when we hear those we love—the voices of friends, children, lovers, and even the sounds made by pets. Music evokes many moods. We are stirred by the cadence of a John Philip Sousa march, a romantic Viennese waltz, the ominous tones of a Wagnerian opera. Whether we play an instrument, join the chorus, or sit in an audience, music delights us. Nature, too, revels in sound—in the mysterious melodies of hump-back whales, the delicacy of wind chimes in the summer's breeze, or the din of waves crashing on a stormy beach.

Scientists tell us that smell is the most evocative sense, and the least appreciated. We don't like to "smell," either actively or passively. Americans devote considerable time and money to neutralize or mask personal body odors, and we think poorly of cultures less intent on deodorizing than we are. Yet, at least subliminally, our sense of smell plays a significant role in our close relationships. Pheromones are distinctive chemical molecules released by each of us that we recognize in one another through our sense of smell. Mothers quickly come to identify the characteristic fragrance of their new baby's skin, and spouses recognize their partner's familiar scent on an item of personal clothing.

We connect with nature through the fragrance of a springtime garden, the scent of newly mowed grass, or even the pungency of a barnyard. Aromas elicit emotions. Think of the homey comfort of fresh baked bread, the solemnity of incense in a monastery chapel, an evocative whiff of perfume. Aromas can literally expand us, leading us to breathe deeply, filling our lungs with oxygen and enhancing our sense of well-being. Some fragrances, such as peppermint, lemon, or eucalyptus, are stimulants that make us more alert. Chamomile, spiced apple, and lavender are among the fragrances that support relaxation by slowing our breathing.

Through taste, we experience the essential pleasure of food—the juicy sweetness of a ripe pear, the distinctive succulence of a home-grown tomato, the airy crunchiness of freshly popped corn, the depth and richness of a fine wine. A drink of cool water on a hot day delights us, as does a steaming cup of cocoa on a winter afternoon. Taste adds to the pleasure we share with those we love, whether through a simple meal prepared for a friend or a gourmet feast celebrating a special family occasion.

Since food is so central to how we care for ourselves and one another, tastes often play a symbolic role. Sweets and starchy foods such as bread and potatoes sometimes become "stand-ins" for nurture and nourishment otherwise lacking to us. There is a biological basis to what we call comfort foods, as pasta, potatoes, and bread are high in carbohydrates. Digesting these foods raises the level of serotonin in the brain and reduces feelings of anxiety.

The pleasures of touch can come through a gentle caress or a supportive hug, a soothing hot bath or an invigorating massage. Some touch is subtle, as in the feel of cool sheets on a hot summer night or the whisper of silk against one's skin. Other touch is more energetic, as when we stroke the luxurious coat of the family pet or knead bread dough. Much of the satisfaction in craft work comes from the feel of the medium: clay and water on a potter's wheel, the textures of thread and fabric in needlework, the grain in the wood that we carve, sand, and polish.

Affectionate touch expresses and strengthens our sense of closeness to those we love. As children, if we are fortunate, we have parents who hold, stroke, and caress us, who wrap us in protective embraces that we will remember long after we have left home. As adults, we experience the caring and comforting touch of a lover, a touch that produces both healing and delight.

JESUS AND THE POWER OF TOUCH

Recalling Jesus' life can help us appreciate the power of touch. In Mark's gospel, we meet a very human Jesus who is frequently in physical contact with other people. At dinner one evening, a woman approaches to anoint Jesus' head with expensive, fragrant oil. This sensual act startles and offends his companions. They attempt to deal with their discomfort over what seems to them unseemly intimacy by arguing about extravagance and waste, but Jesus responds, "Leave her alone!" He welcomes being touched in this way.

Throughout Mark's gospel we read about those who are sick seeking Jesus out. When they find him, Jesus often responds in a way that changes their lives. And Jesus seems to need to touch, to make contact with those who approach him. When he heals a blind man, Jesus mixes dirt with his own spit and presses the mud into the man's eyes; gradually he regains his sight. In other places Jesus responds to the simplicity of children. "And he took them up in his arms, laid his hands on them and blessed them" (Mk 10:16).

In one of the most compelling accounts of Jesus' contact with others, a sick woman approaches him with the conviction that if she can even touch his clothes, she will be healed (Mk 5:28). Jesus comes to a halt, aware that he has been touched in some special way. When he asks who touched him, his friends are surprised, since they have been jostling their way through a crowd. Jesus tells them that he felt power going out of him. There is a lesson here: Touch has the power to heal if we honor its sensual/spiritual force.

FEELINGS THAT MOVE US

Emotions (e-motions) are feelings that move us. Strong feelings are not just private events that happen inside our own skin. Instead, as Carl Jung reminds us, our passions "bind us to others and to the living world." Emotions are social impulses that connect us with other people, communicate our inner experience, and energize our responses. When we embrace our passions, they can move us toward deeper self-awareness; they can also move us out into the world.

Empathy opens us to the depths in other people. Since we, too, have felt anger, arousal, and grief, we can recognize the significance and appreciate the impact of these experiences in the lives of others. Connections like these empower us to respond sensitively to another person's hopes and needs in a way that gives priority to that person's experience. Through empathy, we set aside our own concerns to honor the experiences and values of others—from their perspective. The gentle discipline of self-emptying can develop into genuine mutuality.

Anger rouses us to action, sending out an alarm that something is wrong and must be set right. Anger responds to injury or insult by urging us to move against those who have caused the harm. Anger against injustice can bring people together in fruitful protest that says, "We are many and our cause is just." Sometimes, to be sure, anger's passion misleads us, and we overreact in violence or blame the wrong person. This is why we must learn to tame our anger, examining its claims and evaluating our options before we respond. But, having been purified, anger is an ally that alerts us to genuine threat and fuels our commitment to confront intolerable situations.

Compassion awakens us to other people's pain and to our shared humanity: "This person who suffers is kin to me." In compassion, we are moved by someone else's distress. Sometimes we are moved to tears; more significantly, compassion moves us to act. We respond with rituals of healing, gestures of solidarity, demands for justice.

Guilt can seem very self-focused, but this passion also guards our relationships. Guilt signals that we have given offense, and the distress it causes should move us to seek reconciliation with those we have injured. Guilt calls us to be our best selves; it urges us to reaffirm commitments that give meaning to our lives.

Fidelity strengthens our love. When we recall the promises we have made, fidelity empowers our commitments. When we are hurt by those we love, fidelity moves us toward forgiveness. Conflicts and inconsistencies are inevitably part of any significant relationship, and fidelity makes reconciliation possible.

Devotion empowers our active concern for the well-being of those we love, not just as extensions of ourselves but for their own sake. In devoted love, we consider another person's well-being to be as important as our own. Mutual devotion brings us the cherished gift of being held ourselves in such caring embrace. Devotion is *eros* tested, love that has endured, care that has become a way of life.

Gratitude is a graced awareness of gifts received that moves us to expressions of thanks. It links us in affection with those who have blessed our lives, and makes us generous in return.

Eros moves in these and in all our social emotions. In desire, *eros* motivates our choices and deepens our commitments. In longing, *eros* opens us to the pain and the beauty of the world. In passion, *eros* enriches our lives with sexual pleasure and fruitful love.

EROS AND SEXUAL PASSION

We know from our own lives that sexual passion is volatile and ambiguous. Its energy can turn selfish and sometimes destructive, as impulses we barely understand drive us to hurt other people and abuse ourselves. Erik Erikson describes this danger. "Before genital maturity is reached, much of sexual life is the self-seeking, identity-hungry kind . . . or it remains a kind of genital combat in which each tries to defeat the other."

But experience shows, too, how this ambiguous passion matures. From good friends we learn the rhythms of giving and receiving affection. In marriage we promise our passion to another person and grow stronger by keeping that promise. And, as our hearts expand, strangers—and even those who have harmed us—can arouse our compassion.

The desire for contact and more life floods every part of our embodied selves. The passionate hope to be with another person, to link our lives in fruitful ways, to commit to values beyond ourselves energizes both our sexuality and our spirituality. The complex power of our sexuality comes to us as God's erotic gift. Because our bodily passion is not an enemy or a demon, we do not need to subjugate it. Because our sexual desire is not essentially selfish, abstinence will not be our ordinary discipline. We learn instead to befriend the *eros* of sexuality.

Befriending our sexuality is a lifelong process. As our experience of *eros* expands, connections between emotional attraction, sexual arousal, and devoted love deepen. As we recognize the sensual roots of our emotions and affirm the ways in which sexual passion opens us to another's spirit, our erotic lives become more integrated.

Puberty marks a critical stage on the journey. Suddenly sex looms large. Our bodies are easily aroused and eager for touch. Sexual pleasure beckons, even as the complexities of dating and mating leave us confused. Early on, sex can seem a stranger. But gradually we grow familiar with our own patterns of desire and arousal, of lovemaking and abstinence, of friendship and romance. As *eros* matures, we come to welcome sexuality as a friend.

How does this happen? Falling in love is often the first step. Recognizing how fragile and sometimes risky this "first love" can be, some people—especially parents of teenagers!—are wary of early infatuation, but psychologists consider the experience as crucial. Infatuation hints that sexual attraction and genuine care are not mutually exclusive.

Young love proclaims that passion and friendship are compatible. We are fortunate when our adult experience confirms this early promise. The affection we share with those close to us expresses and deepens our bond. The passion of early romance expands as we discover the links between intimate touch and mutual devotion. We savor this blessing in marriage, as sexual passion matures in our committed love.

As erotic experience becomes more integrated, our sexual lives become more intentional. Sex is not just something that happens to us, largely beyond our control or outside our responsibility. Our sexuality is now more value-laden, shaped by personal discernment and choice. It finds its place among the values and ideals that give meaning to our lives.

We learn along the way that sexual integration is neither automatically nor exclusively available to those who marry. The issue is not whether we are married or single, whether we know ourselves as lesbian, gay, or bi-sexual, or whether we commit ourselves in religious celibacy or in relationships that embrace sexual love. Each of these lifestyles can be gratifying and grace-filled. The challenge for each of us is similar—to embrace ways of living and loving that are generous, faithful, and fruitful.

Embodied Love

The Song of Songs, a lyrical poem about two lovers, encourages us in befriending *eros*. Neither a historical narrative nor a catalogue of laws, it is a poem that celebrates erotic love.

> How beautiful you are, my love,
> How very beautiful!
> Your eyes are doves behind your veil . . .
> Your lips are like a crimson thread
> And your mouth is lovely . . .
> Your two breasts are two fawns . . .
> You are altogether beautiful, my love,
> There is no flaw in you. (Song 4:1, 3, 5, 7)

What are such sexually provocative words doing in our Bible? Scripture scholar Andre LaCocque remarks: "It is a miracle in itself that the Song of Songs is in the canon of Holy Scriptures." How are we to understand it? One interpretation viewed the poem as a dialogue between a bride and her bridegroom. Seeing these lovers as married would make their passion more legitimate. A second interpretation, the favorite for more than two thousand years, regarded the entire book as an allegory of the love between God and the human soul. Thus, a poem about human love was transformed into a treatise on religious devotion.

Recently, scripture scholars have returned to the poem's most obvious meaning, as a celebration of sensual love. As Roland Murphy comments, "The course of events does not appear to be leading anywhere; the lover and beloved are simply enjoying each other's presence and affection." In this interpretation, the ancient poem can symbolize God's passionate love for us only because erotic love is itself good and holy.

> With great delight I sat in his shadow,
> And his fruit was sweet to my taste.

He brought me to the banqueting house,
And his intention toward me was love. (Song 2:3–4)

Christian morality has often made sexuality's goodness dependent on fertility; making love is acceptable when a married
couple intend to have a child. But this poem does not speak of
children; it lingers with delight on the essential goodness of sexual
desire. The poem concludes with a powerful assertion of the link
between human passion and the heart of God.

For love is strong as death,
Passion fierce as the grave.
Its flashes are flashes of fire, a raging flame.
Many waters cannot quench love
Neither can floods drown it. (Song 8:6–7)

Befriending the *eros* of sexuality, we can confirm the biblical
testimony through the experience of our own lives. With its unexpected awakenings and unearned delights, sex echoes God's
gracious creation. Sexual attraction stirs our creativity, draws us to
others, and initiates fruitful life commitments. We recognize, too,
the blessings of sexual pleasure. In the caresses of sexual sharing
we are revealed to ourselves; we come to see a loveliness that we
had been incapable of imagining on our own. We often find spiritual healing in our sexual lives, as our physical embraces soothe
old wounds and make forgiveness tangible. In the intimacy we
share with a beloved sexual partner, the reality of God's goodness
and forgiveness become more than rhetoric. As lovers, we give
thanks for this erotic grace.

FOR FURTHER REFLECTION

Spend time during this week asking yourself these questions, and listen carefully to what your body has to say to you. There are many ways to carry out this exercise: write in your journal, share with a friend, sit quietly in a comfortable place, go for a reflective walk, etc.

What is my body for me at this moment:

A source of delight?

A burden or an obstacle?

A reliable resource?

A temple of the Holy Spirit?

Or...

These days, do I abuse my body in any way?

Why/how does this happen?

Can I recall a time...

...when I have been able to acknowledge the beauty and strengths of my own body?

...when I have been able to accept the needs and limitations of my own body?

...when I have been able to give thanks for my body, as part of my experience of God?

What is my body asking of me now?

How will I respond?

6

Benefits of the Body

STOREHOUSE OF WISDOM AND ENERGY

O Lord, you have searched me and known me . . .
For it was you who formed my inward parts;
You knit me together in my mother's womb.
I praise you, for I am fearfully and wonderfully made.
— Psalm 139

Our bodies are smarter than they look. Consider this ordinary example: I put in a week of long hours at work, pushing against a deadline. Carrying these worries home, I spend restless nights without sleep. Next, a pounding headache or upset stomach adds to my distress. These physical symptoms signal that something is wrong. With medication or willpower I try to override the signal. But as I focus on getting rid of the symptoms, I ignore my body's wisdom. My body recognizes, often before the mind does, my true situation.

In his award-winning novel *Cold Mountain*, Charles Frazier tells the story of a Civil War soldier who is slowly recovering in a military hospital from grievous wounds suffered in combat. After weeks of recuperation the man takes a short walk into the nearby town. His neck wound is slowly mending; his hip still aches from his serious injury. As he walks this wounded soldier reflects on his condition. "All in all, his wounds gave him just reason to doubt that he would ever heal up and feel whole and of a piece again." But as he begins his walk back to the hospital, he realizes that his legs feel "surprisingly sturdy and willing." Willing for what? His legs seem to be telling him he can and should walk away from the war. His days have been filled with waking nightmares of the slaughter he has been part of. As his body begins to heal, it announces that it is time to go home.

Medical science gives further insight into the body's wisdom. The immune system, operating outside our conscious control, alerts the body to hostile intruders and mobilizes a protective response. Research in biology and neurology has also uncovered the wise workings of "the second brain"—the enteric nervous system in the gut, which manages the complicated processes of digestion. Our stomach quickly recognizes spoiled food we have eaten and moves reflexively to expel it. Here too, the body is at work below the level of consciousness, wisely seeing to our well-being.

Yet another kind of "immune system" guards our moral integrity. Chinese scholar Ci Jiwei offers this enigmatic statement: "The body does not know what is moral, but it knows what is not." Knowing what *is* moral demands all our resources—intellectual and instinctual, psychological and spiritual. But we recognize what *is not* moral more intuitively, for example, when we flinch at an offensive remark or instantly step back in the face of an inappropriate gesture.

Sexuality, too, expresses the body's wisdom. Theologian Luke Timothy Johnson says it well:

> Many of us have experienced sexual pleasure as both humbling and liberating, a way in which our bodies know quicker and better than our minds, choose better and faster than our reluctant wills, even get us to where God apparently wants us in a way our minds never could.

If our bodies harbor wisdom, they also store up longings for which we have no name. And we recognize that the body is not quite identical with the "self," but is in some way "other." The body registers desires and laments that bewilder or bedevil us. Sex, for all its intimacy with the body, provides a prime example of this paradox: Our sexuality links us with others while often putting us at odds with ourselves.

Estrangement from the body comes into play in our response to trauma. Many people who have been severely abused in childhood carry no conscious memory of this early ordeal. It is as though the terrible injury is too devastating to acknowledge, especially given the few resources a child has on hand. And so the memory, retained unconsciously, lies buried in the body. There it resides, surfacing at times in the disguise of bodily symptoms. The body remembers what the conscious mind cannot afford to admit.

But often, as the wounded child—now adult—matures, new personal strengths develop. As these resources become available, the "forgotten" memory resurfaces. Having been kept safe these many years in the storehouse of the body, the memory reappears, waiting to be healed.

HONORING THE BODY'S ENERGY

We have identified *eros* as a Western metaphor for our vitality, the ebb and flow of life's energy as we move through our days and our duties. *Ch'i* is the Chinese name for the vital energy that animates the world. Western observers sometimes ask whether *ch'i* is physical energy or a more spiritual force. To most Chinese, that question itself is puzzling. The vitality that enlivens our bodies is the same energy that permeates the universe: what could be more obvious? *Ch'i* is at once physiological and spiritual: It names the energy generated in the body's metabolic activity and carried in our blood; *ch'i* also registers the more subtle shifts of elation and depletion in our mind/heart. Acknowledging this pervasive yet mysterious energy, many phrases in the Chinese language include this word *ch'i*. Anger, for example, becomes "energy rising" (*sheng ch'i*) and the familiar end-of-the-day fatigue is rendered as "evening energy" (*mu ch'i*).

For more than two thousand years the Chinese have developed bodily practices—graceful movements of *tai chi;* breathing disciplines of *qigong*; therapeutic strategies of acupuncture and other techniques of traditional medicine—seeking to better attune their lives to this invigorating force. Such practices are rooted in deep cultural awareness of the integral connections between physical energy and spiritual vitality. And today, many in the West—scientists, health professionals, those on the spiritual journey—are exploring the links between energy and holistic well-being.

Physiologist Robert Thayer has focused his research on the basic bodily rhythms that accompany our experience of vitality. Zest for life, he reports, depends on being able to be both energized and relaxed at the same time. Thayer calls this state of relaxed alertness *calm energy*. His work helps us shape a practical spirituality of *eros*, by alerting us to personal choices and daily practices that enhance personal vitality.

Pain and pleasure are the most dramatic examples of how physical sensations color our consciousness. But our more ordinary experience of daily life is constantly filtered through bodily awareness. Two basic dimensions of our physical condition shape our daily mood—energy and tension. Energy is produced by the natural processes of the body. Digestion, metabolism, sleep, emotional arousal, and physical exercise all work to generate the vitality we need for the daily activities of life. Optimal vitality comes in balancing our body's expenditure and replenishment of energy. And awareness of our energy level—our own sense of vitality—is a reliable gauge of our state of physical health.

Tension registers a state of mind, our awareness of challenge or threat. Tension arises in response to judgments we make about impending events. These negative assessments manifest in our bodies as physiological stress. When we sense danger, our stress level rises to fuel a swift defense. But continued stress exhausts this tense energy and depletes both our strength and our confidence. And the threat that tension registers does not always have to do with an obvious danger in the external environment. Often enough, the threat arises from memories of wounds and inadequacies in our past.

THE RHYTHMS OF EROS—ENERGY AND TENSION

Most of us are familiar with the shifts in our own energy level. Some of us are "morning people," rising early with eagerness to begin the work of the day, but then gradually losing our effectiveness as the day progresses. Others know themselves to be "evening people," those who are slow to get started in the morning and who achieve their best work in the later hours, after routine chores are completed and children have been put to bed.

While people differ in how the day's energy unfolds, we recognize certain familiar patterns. At morning wake-up, many people typically experience their energy at a low ebb. But, for most of us, energy rises quickly—spurred by physical movement, breakfast, and our interest in the day ahead. Characteristically, energy levels reach a high point in late morning or early afternoon. From that elevated level, bodily energy begins to decline to a low point in the middle or late afternoon. For many people, energy increases again—even if only slightly—after the evening meal, and then falls to its lowest point just before bedtime. Not everyone fits this schedule exactly, but most people develop a rhythm of personal energy that remains somewhat constant over time.

This general pattern of alternating energy (the ebb and flow of *eros*) seems to have evolved over earlier millennia, to match the daily rhythm of daylight and darkness. But in our own day the demands of modern life intrude. One career may require regular pre-dawn commuting or long evening meetings; another person's job might include periodic night-shift duties, that play havoc with normal patterns of work and rest. Both external circumstances and emotional stress can disrupt our natural energy rhythm, substituting a tension-filled schedule. The frequent result is a fitful sleep from which we do not awake refreshed. Over time, this self-defeating cycle becomes chronic: A person's energy level is regularly diminished by stressful tension; worry and over-stimulation defy attempts to give ourselves over to replenishing sleep.

CALM ENERGY/CALM TIREDNESS

Calm energy is the physical vitality that supports our engagement with life. We feel alert and active, largely free from the distractions that accumulate with stress. With few negative thoughts clouding our consciousness, we tend to see ourselves in a positive light. This sense of satisfaction sustains our energy in times of busy activity. But positive feelings also make it easier for us to appreciate our body's tiredness. And tiredness, Michel Leunig insists, "is one of our strongest, most noble and instructive feelings; it is an important aspect of our conscience and must be heeded or else we will not survive."

When calm energy predominates, we experience a satisfying rhythm of effort and rest. We are able to enjoy the productive activities we undertake when our energy level is high, and are then able to welcome a satisfying fatigue as energy drains away. At the end of the day we climb into bed, undisturbed by urgent thoughts about things undone or future problems to be confronted. Falling soon into a sound sleep, we awake to move gently into the next day.

Our bodies are designed to produce such calm energy. This essential vitality or *eros* is generated from healthy eating habits, regular physical activity, restorative sleep. Positive emotions also generate calm energy. Happiness, empathy, joy, delight, gratitude, hope—these emotions enhance the levels of serotonin and other endorphins in the bloodstream and contribute to a sense of vital well-being. Psychologist Mihaly Csikszentmihalyi expands our understanding of a particular kind of calm energy that he calls *flow*.

Flow describes those charmed experiences when our attention is absorbed in a deeply satisfying activity. Our focus may be a complex task—performing heart surgery or repairing an engine, writing poetry or crafting furniture, preparing a gourmet meal or solving a puzzle. The task may be athletic—a strenuous mountain climb or a marathon race. Or a person may be absorbed in a game of chess or paying close attention to the simple gestures of soothing a small child. In each instance, the person devotes energy and concentration to the task at hand. But the activity is not experienced as tiring. Instead, the satisfying activity generates a sense of personal vitality.

In flow, we are fully centered: our attention is focused on what we are doing now, with no extraneous thoughts to distract us, no energy wasted in wishing we were doing something else. Typically, activities that generate flow give us a sense of accomplishment but also include an element of challenge. We may feel stretched to bring all our resources into play, but we are ready for the test, eager to confirm and expand our capacity.

A common characteristic of people in the midst of flow is a sense of self-determination. People see their effort—whether in work or at leisure—as something they have personally chosen and as valuable for its own sake. Frequently the task at hand moves toward a goal, but the goal is secondary. Flow comes in being fully involved in the activity itself, not simply in the satisfaction of achieving a result.

In experiences like this, people often lose track of time. Our attention is focused and our concentration is high, so time seems to stand still. But when we look up from the absorbing task, we may find that hours have passed, without leaving us fatigued. We've been expending energy, perhaps even experiencing some tension in our concentrated effort, but the stress has been more energizing than depleting.

TRACKING TENSE ENERGY

Few of us live most of our days in the mood of calm energy. Instead, we frequently face demands that simply consume our energy without any sense of renewal or replenishment. Responsibilities as parents and workers and citizens and friends require that we continue to act even then, when our resources are low. In these situations, other physiological factors—chiefly anxiety and stress—come into play.

Most of us recognize the connections between energy and stress. Preparing for a critical meeting or starting a difficult task, we feel both energized and alert. Early on these dynamics seem complementary—serotonin and adrenaline working together to heighten both our concentration and our mood. But gradually our awareness shifts, as alertness is transformed into anxiety. This shift often registers in our thoughts even before we sense that our muscles are growing tight or stiff. We become increasingly self-critical, or more easily irritated by others. Our interpretations of current events and future possibilities turn sour. Negative emotions—anger, fear, self-doubt, jealousy, envy—begin to predominate, as the adrenal system supplies emergency energy to ready us for self-defense. Over time our energy resources are exhausted, but the physiological tension in our body does not diminish. Now stress becomes *dis*tressing, as our anxiety level and energy level move in opposite directions.

Usually stress is at a very low level when we awake—at least on our good days! But then we start to face the predictable demands and unexpected challenges that are part of our busy lives. As we confront these events through the morning, our nervous system goes on alert, releasing stress hormones that prepare us for fight-or-flight. Many people count on this physiological surge to get started on the day; some of us even find it exhilarating. But tension mounts as the day progresses, reaching its maximum in late afternoon—when natural energy resources are most likely to be depleted. Stress often continues into the evening hours, especially if our physical energy is not revived by a nourishing evening meal and some time for relaxation. By day's end we are exhausted, but restful sleep eludes us.

TENSE TIREDNESS

Tense tiredness is a familiar feeling. It also ranks among the most unpleasant. Tense tiredness can affect us at any time, yet it usually arises when we still have work to do! So we soldier on, becoming more and more tired and more and more tense. To overcome this "energy crisis," we seek out short-term remedies that will, at least momentarily, shift our sorry mood. These days both legal and illegal drugs are available to boost energy and enhance a sense of well-being. But most of us turn to simpler solutions—cigarettes, coffee and other high-caffeine drinks, sugary snacks. These interventions work for a while, prompting our bodies to produce yet more tense energy. But the stimulating effects are short-lived; as the artificial energy flags, we are left tired but still "wired."

In such a state of fatigue, we come to the close of the day with our resources depleted but our tension level still high. And though we fall into bed exhausted, we can't fall asleep. Continuing physiological stress keeps our body on alert. How are we to "come down"? Now the artificial stimulants that kept us going through an exhausting day must be replaced by other interventions. And here the pharmaceutical companies and alcohol industries stand ready to serve. But experience shows that the alcoholic beverages that initially help us feel relaxed do not usher us into reliably restful sleep. And most commercial sleep-aids do not support the deep levels of sleep we need if we are to awake genuinely rested. From a night of tense tiredness we awake still feeling depleted, and so the cycle begins again.

WHAT ARE WE TO DO?

We may admit that calm energy, and the experiences of vital *eros* and joy that accompany this experience of vitality, seem in short supply. But many will insist: The practical demands of life with long work days, accompanied by high stress and little relief, are non-negotiable. "There is nothing I can do!"

Recovering calm energy starts with recognizing the power of physical exercise to overcome stress. As the body moves, tension begins to dissipate; this is how we are designed. Even brief exertion—walking up a flight of stairs rather than taking the elevator; a few moments spent in stretching out muscles in the arms and legs and back; parking the car at some distance from the building entrance so a short walk is required—can begin a process of calming.

Even more powerful is the practice of mindful breathing. Focusing attention on the bodily rhythm of inhaling and exhaling, or using a gentle count to slow the flow of breath—such simple efforts help clear our minds of the mental and emotional distractions that tense energy provokes. These ordinary strategies—physical exertion and focused breathing—are easily available and almost always effective as a quick release from tense energy.

But lifestyle responses have more lasting results. These effective life strategies begin in self-awareness, in recognizing our own patterns of energy and tension. We might start to pay attention to our daily energy cycles. We can learn from our successes and our failures in responding to tension and incorporate what we have learned into our daily life patterns. With this information, we can move more confidently toward commitments that support calm energy.

Lifestyle responses will include paying closer attention to what we eat and to how different foods affect us. Calm energy is the biological product of proper nutrition—eating a balanced diet of different foods, in small portions, at regularly spaced intervals throughout the day. Most of us do have some control over what and when we eat, even if we don't always exercise that control. Decreasing the amount of coffee and caffeinated drinks we consume each day, substituting whole grain breads and cereals for sugary breakfast foods, and enjoying fresh fruit for desserts will contribute mightily to a calmer, more energetic life. Here again systematic self-observation is important, because foods affect different people differently.

A commitment to exercise is perhaps the most effective life strategy in support of calm energy. Physical activity is both toner and tranquilizer, raising energy levels and dissipating tension. A regular exercise program provides multiple benefits: developing muscle tone, improving digestion, helping control weight, and providing mental release. Physical exercise, then, serves both as an emergency stress release and as a regular component of a healthy lifestyle. But to reap these obvious benefits, people need to find an exercise program that is actually enjoyable. "If it isn't fun while you are doing it, you won't stick with it," Robert Thayer cautions. "Many people begin with programs that are too difficult, because they want to see fast results. Unfortunately, these people quit even though they get into shape and feel great for a short while. I think that the reason they quit . . . is that their exercise programs are just too onerous."

Getting enough sleep is an often-neglected life strategy that supports calm energy. While it is true that people differ in how much sleep they need, research indicates that many Americans these days are "sleep deprived." For most adults, waking refreshed seems to require seven to eight hours of uninterrupted sleep on a regular basis. But adults usually report sleep patterns that fall far short of this average. Dependence on pharmaceutical assistance is now routine for many people, whether they seek that assistance for help in falling asleep or help in staying awake. These artificial interventions interfere with the body's natural sleep patterns. Normal rhythms of alert wakefulness and calm tiredness are disrupted, even as the effectiveness of the sleep-aids gradually diminishes. Denied the benefits of restorative sleep, the body awakens already tense. Throughout the day that follows, calm energy remains in short supply.

Stress management techniques of meditation, *tai chi*, yoga, massage, even a hot bath can calm the body and help restore a sense of well-being. With regular practice these strategies enhance calm energy by helping us control anxiety-producing thoughts and stay focused in our commitments to care for our embodied self.

The Jewish and Christian traditions have been keenly aware of the body as a wordless source of both prayer and puzzlement. A bodily longing can become a prayer, a reminder of the soul's yearning for solace and nourishment. As Paul reminded his community, "the Spirit helps us in our weakness; we do not know how to pray as we ought, but that very Spirit intercedes with sighs too deep for words" (Rom 8:26). Our sighs, like the psalmist's bodily aches, may register a wordless longing for God who is our source.

FOR FURTHER REFLECTION

Select a quiet time for this brief meditation.

Begin by sitting in a comfortable position and taking a
moment to let your breathing settle into a slower rhythm.

Then become present to your body; come home to your
body. Let yourself settle here. Gently greet each part
of your body, without judgment and with the greatest
respect.

Now bring your attention inside your body and notice
any heavy sensations here (an ache in the abdomen,
tightness in the chest, tiredness in the back, strain
across the shoulders, cramping in the neck).

Notice any delightful sensations as well (softness in the
belly, expansiveness in the heart, alertness in the spine,
relaxation in the face, warmth in the hands). Just lovingly
notice.

As you breathe in, cup your hands to gather all these
sensations up like a handful of flower petals. As you
breathe out, open your hands to release these sensations
. . . letting them dissolve, letting them go

Now move further into your body-self and notice
what emotions are there, both positive feelings and
troublesome feelings. As you breathe in, gather these
up like a handful of flower petals and as you breathe out,
release them and let them go.

Now move deeper still into your own body-person and
notice your thoughts, both those that console and those

that distress you. As you breathe in, gather up the petals of your thoughts, and as you breathe out, release them. Offer them as a gift to the One who knows all, blesses all, receives all unconditionally.

Now sit quietly in the monastery of your body and listen to the sounds of silence. Then bring your meditation to a close with the psalmist's prayer:

> *O Lord, you have searched me and known me.*
> *You know when I sit down and when I rise up;*
> *You discern my thoughts from far away...*
> *For it was you who formed my inward parts;*
> *You knit me together in my mother's womb.*
> *I praise you, for I am fearfully and wonderfully*
>   *made. (Ps 139)*

7

Befriending Our Bodies

LOVELY, LIMITED, HOLY

The first inner territory of the spiritual journey is the body.
— Theologian Jack Shea

Christians in America hear harsh judgments about our bodies from both religion and culture. Influenced by the traditional dichotomy of flesh and spirit, many Christians have learned to disparage their own bodies. American culture advertises a schizophrenic view of the human body: the body beautiful—and the health products and cosmetic regimes that attend to it—is much extolled, but we are constantly reminded that our own bodies fall deplorably short of this ideal.

BODY IMAGE AND HOW IT DEVELOPS

Body image is the inner view of the outer self. Each of us carries an interior sense of our physical appearance, an awareness that is seldom identical with what we see in a photograph. Often a considerable gap exists between how we view our bodies and how they look to others. Frequently the gap is reinforced by our own negative judgments.

Body image emerges from a complex combination of information, attitudes, feelings, and values. In America's health-conscious society, for example, much of the information about our bodies is

77

recorded in numbers. We know our age, height, weight, and clothing size. Many of us can also report our blood-pressure range, our cholesterol count ("good" and "bad"), our body-mass fat ratio, and our aerobic stress level.

These numbers represent only a part of our body image. The physical facts about our bodies are always interpreted through our expectations. What do I *want* to look like? What is my *ideal* weight, my *best* athletic performance, my *preferred* skin tone? Many adults carry a conscious perception of multiple defects in their physical appearance. Women tend to be more critical of their bodies than men, but dissatisfaction is registered by both. The sense of "how I feel about my body" is basic to our body image.

This interior image of our bodies is a personal construct that is significantly shaped by cultural values. In contemporary U.S. society, for example, standards of physical fitness, sexual vigor, youthfulness, thinness, and glamour prevail, and global media carry these physical standards across the world. Unrealistic ideals intensify our personal dissatisfaction and expand the worldwide market for cosmetics and pharmaceuticals.

Body image is often disconnected from objective information. In fact, studies show that there is little relationship between the actual physical attractiveness of a person's body and his or her satisfaction with it. But there is a strong relationship between body image and self-esteem.

With advances in prenatal care, parents often learn the sex of their baby early in pregnancy. Even before the child's birth, parents relate to him or her in terms of gender. Clothes and toys are selected with gender in mind, and in America, even color preferences are guided by gender—pink for girls, blue for boys. Parents' hopes and expectations, along with their child-rearing practices, are frequently shaped by the culture's images of "the good girl" and "the real boy."

Sometimes these expectations are communicated to the child in messages of bodily shame or physical inadequacy: the boy who is not "strong and tough," the girl who is not "petite and pretty," or who can never be the son her parents really wanted. A child with a physical disability can be particularly vulnerable. One of our friends tells of how the response provoked by the artificial leg he began to wear in his twenties (which generated sympathy, admiration, and often positive curiosity) differed greatly from people's attitudes toward him during his childhood, when he walked with a limp. Then he was seen as deformed and shunned as a cripple.

Adolescence is a critical time in the development of body image. Over the four years or so of puberty, both girls and boys experience dramatic changes in body shape and weight. These changes are evaluated differently. Boys are usually eager for the physical changes, proud to watch their bodies grow stronger and expanding muscles fill out their physique. As their voices deepen and beard growth begins, adolescent boys move closer to the cultural icon of masculinity. For some adolescent girls, too, changing body shape is welcome; they feel more sexy, more attractive to men. For many adolescent girls, however, growing into a woman's larger body, with its feminine shape and weight gains, is evaluated negatively. Dieting is a preoccupation of young women (and many who are not young!) in U.S. culture; evidence suggests that two-thirds of girls between thirteen and eighteen years of age are actively trying to lose weight, and the process of conscious dieting starts for girls at younger and younger ages.

For both boys and girls in adolescence, body awareness is sometimes cloaked with embarrassment, even shame. The tallest girl, the shortest boy, an early development of breasts, a late appearance of facial hair—these anomalies set teenagers apart from their peers. Society's conflicted messages complicate young people's struggle to understand and accept themselves as sexual persons. Genital arousal, penis erection, menstruation, and nocturnal emission can occur unexpectedly, suggesting that an adolescent's body is somehow beyond the person's control. Sometimes parents' warnings and religious prohibitions reinforce the sense that the body cannot be trusted. A single man in his late twenties remembers,

I went through puberty at age eleven. That was pretty young and very awkward for me. I was the first in my class to go through this transformation. The difficulty was compounded by the fact that I had no strong male model in my life and that women were the main teachers in the school that I attended. So the questions that I had about going through puberty were left unanswered. . . . At first, I began to seek out people to talk to about what I was experiencing. I quickly learned that men in our society don't talk about such things! As a result, my body image and my image of myself have always been pretty low. Friends in my life have told me that I'm a wonderful person, but I have never believed them. I have always seen myself as ugly, fat, and troll-like. I have learned that the questions I had as a teenager were normal. I've also discovered that how I am put together, emotionally and physically, is okay!

Psychologists today use the term *emerging adulthood* to describe a new phase in young adult experience. People in their twenties and early thirties recognize that they are no longer adolescents, but many see themselves as not-yet-adult. They are still experimenting with career, relationships, finances, and life values. Some continue to live in their parents' home, but most have established separate—and frequently changing—residences. Increasingly, young people remain unmarried through their twenties or longer, although many have sexual partners with whom they share living arrangements. These young people recognize and protect their independence from their families of origin, but unlike the young adults of the 1960s, few see themselves as revolutionaries or dropouts from society. Instead, they are delaying the significant commitments of love (marriage and, especially, parenthood) and career until they have more experience.

For many young adult women, body image remains dominated by increasingly oppressive cultural ideals of thinness, sexiness, and glamour. Some continue to invest time and money in trying to conform to these cultural norms, while others recognize their arbitrariness and struggle to establish personal standards that make more sense. Many young adult men also have a heightened concern about body image, which more often focuses on "the myth of masculinity" and emphasizes physical prowess in athletics and sexual performance.

Young adults face compelling questions about the role of sexual activity in their lives. How significant is sex? What values motivate sexual activity, and what criteria should govern the choice of a partner? What are the implications of sexual behavior now for health, self-esteem, relationships, and commitments in the future? The desire to start a family grows stronger as men and women move through young adulthood. Married career women as well as single women become more conscious of the "biological clock." Aware that pregnancy after age thirty-five involves increased risks for both mother and child, women confront questions of fertility and parenthood with increasing urgency. For many men in their thirties, personal goals also shift as the desire for parenthood assumes greater priority.

Physical development peaks in our twenties and thirties. As we move through our forties and fifties, our bodies and social relationships begin to change again, and now we are more conscious of the consequences. David Karp reminds us that "the fact of aging seems to be one of life's great surprises, a surprise that is most fully sprung in our fifties." The advertising industry compounds this awareness by cataloging the diminishments that threaten us and then offering cosmetic, surgical, and self-help remedies.

Many midlife adults experience *physique anxiety*. For most men, the focus is strength and stamina, as previous levels of physical performance are out of reach. A father who enjoyed teaching his son to wrestle now finds that his teenager easily excels him. The simple tasks of household maintenance—installing storm windows, mowing the lawn, shoveling snow—have become more physically demanding. His sports activity switches from basketball to the more leisurely pace on the golf course.

Midlife women are often concerned about losing their youthful beauty. A woman's social status depends on her appearance more than a man's does. Women in their late forties seem to experience the highest levels of anxiety over this loss. Younger women may still hold themselves accountable to society's narrow criteria of feminine beauty, but keeping their anxiety at bay requires strenuous exercise, expensive cosmetics, and even surgery. By the time most women reach their fifties, they have come to accept, perhaps even to appreciate, their new physical realities. Carolyn Heilbrun suggests that not until they reach their fifties do most women stop being "female impersonators" and come to embrace the actual persons they now know themselves to be.

Physical change continues during our sixties, seventies, and beyond. Gerontologists, who study the patterns of normal aging, assure us that for most people in developed societies today, the physical changes that accompany aging do not limit daily activities or lifestyles until the late seventies and eighties. Good nutrition, regular exercise, mental stimulation, supportive relationships, and the presence of good friends all help to delay or diminish the negative impact of physical and social changes for older adults.

Psychologically, the reality of our own aging emerges gradually. When we are in our twenties, aging is an alien concept. We know that we belong to a species in which every member grows old and dies, but in practical daily consciousness, growing older "does not apply to me." Often aging makes its initial claims in our thirties, but these encroachments are fleeting. Waking up after a late night party or a missed night's sleep due to work or a sick child, a thirty-five-year-old may look in the mirror and exclaim, "I really look tired!" but the next day, after a good night's sleep, one can look in the mirror and feel that it again reflects "the real me." A decade later, my aging is less a stranger, and the mirror more regularly reports the shifts that come with age. Moving through the fifties, most of us insist that "I don't *feel* old!" even as we recognize the recurring messages that we are, in fact, growing older. As our sixties approach, these facts of personal aging can less easily be overlooked, and by the time we reach our seventies and eighties, aging is an accustomed component of daily life and future planning.

The invitation at all life stages is to befriend our embodied selves. To a lifelong discipline of self-acceptance, the senior years bring the resource of responsible renunciation. We practice discernment amidst life's changes, holding onto the mature strengths of body and spirit that are available to us now, even as we face real diminishments. We learn to grieve with grace, honoring the parts of our past selves that must be let go as we reaffirm our lives now, on the other side of these losses. Western culture's association of beauty with youth complicates our efforts to befriend our aging bodies. A different perspective is offered by the Japanese notion of *shibui,* a word that can be used to describe the rich taste of an aged tea, the subdued beauty of a winter landscape, and the etched lines in an older person's face. This beauty reflects the unique personality that can be crafted only over time.

THE BODY AS SYMBOL

Our bodies are more than mute matter, more than mere flesh and bones. They speak for us in groans and sighs; they speak to us in our aches and our arousals. Our physical appearance and demeanor—tall or broad, awkward or graceful—tell the world something about us. Breaking into a sweat is often more than just a physical expression, as it can represent a response to a sudden psychological or spiritual threat. Most especially our bodily gestures— a slight bow to someone we respect, a comforting hand on the shoulder of a distressed friend—communicate concerns of the heart and express spiritual meanings.

Our erotic bodies are symbolic in three distinctive ways, each announcing to us—and to the world—what our body is and what it is for. These are the enduring images of our bodies as ornamental, as instrumental, and, if we are fortunate, as sacramental.

The Body Ornamental

We love to adorn our bodies, whether with war paint or eyeliner. Through the use of jewelry—from a simple wedding band to an ornate tiara—or of body art—from body piercing to tattoos—we demonstrate our fascination with ornaments. We delight in accessorizing our bodies, highlighting and calling attention to them. Through these adornments we show off, celebrating who we are and what we aspire to become.

Displays of physical adornment are not unique to our species. Similar types of displays are apparent throughout the animal kingdom. Think of the cardinals building their nest in the backyard— the males adorned with striking red feathers, in sharp contrast to the somewhat drab females. Even more extravagant is the peacock with his flamboyant multicolored display.

Other cardinals, these not in the backyard but in Rome, witness to the human and even religious need for ornamental presentation. During the television coverage of the funeral of Pope John Paul II, the whole world viewed the gathered clerics resplendent in their finery. This medieval pageantry reminded us of the deep human desire to decorate our bodies, broadcasting messages about ourselves through ornamentation. All these displays are about *eros*.

Many of us remember connections between religion and ornamentation. For example, as Easter approached at the end of the long Lenten season, a mother would buy a new hat for herself and some special article of clothing for each of the children. (Fathers often seemed exempt from this annual display!) On Easter Sunday, candles and a vibrant display of flowers filled the sanctuary. The lesson we learned—even for those of us living in still-frozen Minnesota's long wait for spring—was that Easter is a time for ornamentation. Just before the beginning of Lent, the penitential season preceding Easter, Mardi Gras festivities—with their gaudy masks, provocative costumes, and "over-the-top" physical display— provide a social stage for the body ornamental. At both ends of the Lenten season we are reminded that Christian culture itself is attuned to the vitality of ornamentation.

Even in a text as old as the biblical Song of Songs, our religious heritage recognized ornamenting the body as part of holy *eros*. "Your cheeks are beautiful with ornaments, your neck with strings of jewels. We will make you ornaments of gold, studded with silver" (Song 1:10–11).

In contemporary culture, ornamenting the body can quickly become merely superficial. Various aspects of life—dress, diet, exercise—are recruited into an obsession with ornamenting ourselves. Yet this impulse seems to be an essential part of who we are. In our teens and young adult years, we are especially attuned to the body ornamental. *Eros* is alive in this period of dating and mating when we want to look our best. Later, as we join our lives with those of others in love and work, we may sense a shift in how we perceive our bodies and present them to the world.

The Body Instrumental

> God of power and might, may I grow in strength and courage to use my body—bones and muscles—for the good of your people and all of creation. (Carl Koch and Joyce Heil, *Created in God's Image*)

As we move through our thirties and forties, we will likely come to a richer appreciation of our bodies as instruments that demand constant tuning and protection. Wearing a warm winter jacket becomes more important than maintaining a sleek profile. We recognize nutritious food is a source of the stamina we need to meet the promises we have made, so concern for our diet focuses on staying healthy more than on staying slim. The body, still sturdy, now requires more attention. Even in the heart of our erotic lives, we learn new lessons about the body instrumental. Pregnancy distorts the body, bringing discomfort and the pain of childbirth. Child-rearing, with its sleepless nights and physical demands, tests our strength and stamina.

For all of us, midlife brings a richer appreciation of the body as instrument, as our basic tool to "get things done." If we played sports in our youth, we likely came to some early appreciation of the instrument that is our body, as its agility, strength, and balance enhanced our performance. Some professions, too, give special consideration to the body as a critical instrument of success: professional dancers train and tune their bodies as both instruments and ornaments. Others—medical surgeons, military recruits—depend on the disciplined body to achieve their goals. To meet the demands of our expanding responsibilities, we need to keep this essential equipment in working order. Diet, rest, and exercise become more important in our care for our bodies.

The Body Sacramental

Our bodies are meant to be both ornaments and instruments; and, beyond these, we can recognize a yet richer sense of our bodily selves. Our first recognition may come in lovemaking, as our bodies—for all their awkward limitations—become gifts to be shared and signs of a love that goes beyond words. When lovemaking produces a child we are astonished that our bodies have brought forth new life. On a more prosaic level, we end a full, productive week of work exhausted and grateful that we have not become sick or injured, that we have had the energy and concentration to do good work. In all these experiences we may find our bodies touched by grace and give thanks.

A sacrament is an occasion of grace, a ritual gesture or physical action through which we enter more deeply into the presence of God. In traditional Catholic understanding, the sacraments—such as Eucharist or reconciliation—effect what they signify. In our many gestures of care and compassion, our humble bodies become signs of God's embodied love.

If it was in religious ritual where some of us first recognized the body as ornamental—the priest garbed in brilliant vestments or the choir arrayed in splendid robes—it can also have been in the ritualized gestures of liturgy that we sensed our own bodies as sacramental. A man reflects back on the delights of being an altar boy: "Mass was the ballet of my youth.... [This was] a world where your body was less visible but where your movement was more noticeable." The ornamental clothing of the worship service covers the ministers' bodies, even as the solemn gestures of ritual make them more obvious. "Within these sacred robes, an altar boy's body became a stage prop. Even a young, shapeless youth could feel in his flesh that his movement was grand and dramatic. The bows, the genuflections, the well-timed turns—all these were part of a great sacred drama."

Religious scholar Cristina Traina traces the connections between the body and our sacramental heritage: "It is only in and through the body that we experience grace; therefore the body has sacramental significance." She continues,

We wash, and we are baptized; we eat and we partake of Eucharist; we touch to heal. . . . Our tradition also teaches that in marriage the union of bodies is a sign and symbol of grace that is really present.

In everyday life, our bodies become sacramental through thoughtful practices. We prepare a meal with care to share with family or friends, and food becomes more than fuel. We become more open to God's presence through mindful breathing and centered awareness. We pray with our body, through gesture and song and dance. Many of us today experience the sacramental nature of massage, an expression of respectful touch that weds the sensual and the spiritual. We are anointed with oil as our bodies are stroked with respectful care, in an act reminiscent of the anointing that is part of our sacramental heritage. This sensual anointing brings a relaxing calm or perhaps enlivens us with renewed vigor. On more somber occasions, this holy touch rehearses the final anointing at the end of our days. Here, too, the body becomes a sacrament.

FOR FURTHER REFLECTION

Stand with your weight equally distributed between both feet. Soften the legs and allow them to receive the weight of your body. Let go of all holding; stand with ease; breathe easily and trust.

Draw your hands in prayer to your heart, bowing your head gently:

"My Lord and My God."

Slowly raise your joined hands upwards to the heavens and open your palms to face outward to the world, full of praise for all the ways in which the world proclaims the glory of God:

"I will raise my hands in the holy place
and praise you, O God."

Begin your descent to the earth. Hinge forward from the hips, extend your arms out in front of you. Then let your upper body fold over your lower body until your hands touch the floor in front of you. Continue descending by bending the knees and moving into a squatting position; bow your head:

> *"My whole being bows down in worship before you,*
> *my Lord and my God;*
> *stoop down to touch me and to heal me."*

Slowly uncurl by straightening your legs and rolling smoothly upwards like a flower growing toward the light:

> *"You are my light and my salvation."*

Repeat by opening your arms like the two wings of a bird and extending them above your head, reaching up again in praise:

> *"I will raise my hands in the holy place*
> *and praise you O God."*

Slowly bring your hands to the prayer position, and bow:

> *Amen.*

You can repeat this upward/downward movement as a mantra as often as you wish, noticing that praise and prostration are all one movement, one rhythm, one dance, one prayer.

8

The Eros of Pleasure

PATHWAY TO PRESENCE AND GRATITUDE

It is God who is at work in you, enabling you
both to will and to work for God's good pleasure.
— Philippians 2:13 (authors' translation)

For Christians, Paul announces to the Philippians, the life of faith expresses God's good pleasure. Writing to the community in Ephesus, Paul returns to this conviction: God's plan of salvation is being carried out "according to God's good pleasure set forth in Christ" (Eph 1:9). The Hebrew prophets, too, gave testimony to divine pleasure: God's word, like the rain that waters the fields, "will not return to God unfulfilled, before having carried out God's good pleasure" (Isa 55:11). But pleasure, especially sensual pleasure, has been a stumbling block for many Christians.

The place of pleasure in our spiritual lives is influenced by our starting point. If the spiritual journey begins at the foot of the cross, we honor the redemptive significance of suffering as it has been transformed by Jesus' life and death. From this vantage point, suffering is a privileged pathway to holiness. Christians will soberly seek salvation in the midst of the sinful world. On such a search there is neither time nor place for the dangerous delights of sensual pleasure.

But if our spiritual journey begins with creation, as does the Bible itself, pleasure appears in a different light. God's creation, wounded as it is by violence and evil, still sparkles with beauty.

89

Extravagant colors, enchanting sounds, and fragrant aromas delight us, reinforcing God's own judgment that "it is good." The simple testimony of our senses convinces us that we are designed for pleasure. From this alternate vantage point, pleasure appears less as a scandal and more as a sacrament.

But the puzzle of pleasure endures. Pleasure's intimate association with addiction and violence undermines our confidence. Pleasure's gifts—the fragile delights of our senses, the passion we share in sexual love—soon seem suspect. How does sensual pleasure find its honorable place in Christian spirituality? Can pleasure serve as pathway to a passionate God?

Our religious ancestors were keenly aware of pleasure's temptations. Living in the midst of the hedonism and decadence of the Roman Empire, early Christians struggled to affirm the goodness of the body and its sensual delights. In the fourth century, Augustine described his concern about the pleasures of food. "In eating, a snare of concupiscence is laid for me in that very process, for the passage itself is pleasurable. . . . In eating and drinking, a dangerous pleasure makes itself my companion."

Two hundred years before Augustine, Clement of Alexandria composed a rule to guide the Christian community in North Africa. Acutely aware of the abusive sexual practices rampant in the public baths, Clement advised that Christians might bathe for purposes of hygiene, but not for pleasure. Puzzled by the problem of pleasure, Clement could not call on the experience that many of us cherish today: the sensual delight of a hot bath at the end of a long day of work or worry. As warm water loosens aching muscles, prayer springs spontaneously to our lips: "Thank you, Lord. Thank you." Such a movement from pleasure to prayer was alien to many of our religious ancestors. But for many Christians today, this heritage of suspicion stands at odds with personal experience.

Genuine Pleasure Makes Us Present

What then are we to make of pleasure? What gift does sensual enjoyment bring to the journey of faith? Perhaps the most important gift of pleasure is also the most humble: pleasure makes us present. We live our days distracted by both the past and the future. Past failures and recent mistakes plague us with guilt; challenges await in the coming weeks, making us anxious. Little energy is left simply to be present *now*. Often it is pleasure that bring us back into the here-and-now, making us present again to our lives.

Personal examples may help. A colleague shared with us this story:

> Several years ago a friend gave me a gift, arranging for me to receive a massage from a staff member at his health club. One wintry day, I drove out to the facility with some trepidation. The establishment was certainly reputable, but I still had some misgivings about disrobing and giving over my body to unknown hands. I was introduced to the massage therapist—Ivan—and learned that he had only recently arrived from Russia. Apprehension grew into panic as I conjured up memories of Ivan the Terrible! Almost immediately I noticed that Ivan's wrists appeared thicker than my biceps. But, when his hands began to work the taut muscles of my neck and shoulders, my fear began to give way to pleasure. As his hands kneaded my left arm, its tendons and muscles began to release. Suddenly I became aware of my arm, as I had never been aware of it before. This unnoticed part of my anatomy, faithful servant by my side for more than half a century, was for the first time being acknowledged and honored. The pleasure of this respectful massage startled me into sudden recognition—now I was present to my arm, conscious of it and grateful for it.

Or recall the taste of a truly delicious peach—not the standard supermarket variety, protected by preservatives to assure a six-month shelf life, but a peach from a small organic farm rushed for sale to the local farmer's market. Holding the peach, you feel its slightly resilient firmness. Biting through the skin, sweet juices flood your mouth. So this is what a real peach tastes like! In this moment, your attention is riveted in this delight. The pleasure makes you present.

Or, driving home after a busy day at work, you turn a corner that gives a sudden view of the western sky. This route is familiar territory, and usually you spend the time reworking the day's affairs or planning the evening's events. Today, the sunset grabs your attention, as you are confronted by an array of vivid colors splashed across the horizon. Pulling to the side of the road, you sit for several moments, fully present to this dazzling display. No space here for regret, no call for advance planning—simply presence. The simple pleasures of touch and taste and sight do not remove us from the world but rather intensify our awareness of it.

A counter-example reinforces the link between pleasure and presence. A friend telephones you one morning, inviting you to stop by her apartment that day briefly for a quick lunch. Having discovered a new soup recipe, she has spent several hours preparing the vegetables, simmering the stock, and adding herbs. It has been weeks since the two of you have had any time together; accepting her invitation will accomplish two goals—lunch and conversation. So, reluctant at first (remembering your hectic schedule), you promise to join her around noon. But your eleven o'clock meeting runs way too long. When it's finally finished, you rush over to your friend's apartment. You apologize for arriving so late and, aware of the work waiting for you at the office, you hurriedly consume the meal your friend has set out. As you are preparing to leave, she asks: "How was the soup?" For a moment you panic: The soup? The soup? Then your well-honed social skills kick in: "The soup—" you exclaim, "yes, the soup! It was wonderful, delicious. I loved the soup!"

To tell the truth, of course, you hardly tasted the soup. As you sat at your friend's table, your mind was far away. The morning meeting still concerned you and you were anxious about the afternoon's work. The pleasure of the soup, your friend's special gift, was meant to nourish you and draw you into her presence. But distraction defeated the pleasure. You simply were not "there."

The link between pleasure and presence serves as a reminder to us: Christian spirituality is about presence. We struggle to be present to God's gifts and invitations. We long to be more present to our friends and loved ones, mindful of how easily we neglect them and take them for granted. We aspire to be more alert to our inner spirit, with its fragile hopes and frequent misgivings. Spirituality invites us to be fully alive; being fully alive involves becoming more available, more present—to ourselves, to others, to the Spirit's action in God's world.

The sacramental rituals of the Christian tradition—involving bread and wine, incense and oil, colorful clothes and sensuous sounds—prompt our awareness of God's presence. The sacraments use our senses to bring us in contact with this elusive mystery. In solemnity and celebration, religious rituals proclaim that the sensual and the spiritual were made for each other. Pleasure is the medium; presence is the goal.

GIFTS OF GENUINE PLEASURE

Genuine pleasure nourishes us. Superficial delights can serve as distractions from the labor and boredom of life. But the pleasures of sight and taste and touch are designed for much more. Consider a meal shared with friends or family to celebrate a birthday or anniversary or homecoming. This is no fast-food event. Instead we take time to enjoy each other's company. The pleasure of this meal nourishes us far beyond the calories consumed. When we go too long without such celebrations, our spirits begin to starve.

If the communion of shared meals nurtures us, so too does touch. Physical contact—a comforting embrace, a playful cuddle, a gentle caress—heals our spirit. Novelist Saul Bellows describes a man who goes to the barbershop weekly, not because his hair has grown too long, but because he needs to be touched. Research on premature infants has found that daily exposure to a parent's skin—suckling at the mother's breast or lying on the father's bare chest—enhances the child's physical growth.

Caring touch nourishes and nurtures us. But in American culture today we are keenly aware that touch can be abused. Sexual molestation and pedophilia have been epidemic in Christian churches and elsewhere. As ministers and teachers and counselors, we continue to learn about the boundaries between healthy touch and manipulative intrusions into others' lives. But with today's heightened sensitivity, many caregivers lament that they no longer dare to hug a distressed person, lest this caring gesture be misinterpreted. Anglican priest Jim Cotter writes of the discipline that must protect our touches: "To discern when and how to touch and be touched is an ascetical task: to live by the Spirit is neither not to touch, so hating the flesh, nor to touch indiscriminately, which takes no account of the other."

Recognizing the signs of genuine pleasure helps resolve some of its ambiguity. If pleasure simply distracts without making us more present to our lives, if it tightens our grasp rather than opening us in generosity, if it diminishes us or others rather than strengthening our spirit, then such pleasure may be a moving away from more abundant life.

A second gift of pleasure is gratitude, which flows easily into generosity. At a coffee break in the midst of a long conference, a friend rubs your tense shoulders. "Thank you, thank you!" you respond. And almost spontaneously you are eager to return the favor: "Let me rub your back, too."

This dynamic describes the pleasure of the delicious peach, as well. First I enjoy the peach myself, for the pleasure of its taste. Then I extend my hand to you, wanting to share this delight: "Taste this peach!" The pleasure itself makes me generous. Sharing this sensual delight would seem to subtract from my joy, but it does not diminish my pleasure. In fact, sharing introduces a deeper delight. Witnessing your enjoyment magnifies my pleasure. Here we learn one of life's happiest lessons: Sharing pleasure can be richer and more gratifying than experiencing pleasure alone.

In *The Four Loves*, C. S. Lewis distinguishes between two important experiences of delight: pleasures of need and pleasures of appreciation. Need-pleasures, Lewis suggests, are urgent and instinctual; they impel us to quick satisfaction. Working several hours under a hot sun, for example, we experience a sharp desire for water. As we quench our thirst, we feel a deep satisfaction and our need is quickly extinguished. This experience of pleasure focuses on very specific biological needs. The need is so rapidly satisfied that we speak of it in the past tense—"That was really good!"

Pleasures of appreciation are less urgent and less instinctual. They have to do with satisfactions of the mind and spirit. An example is the pleasure we experience when we come upon a field of wild flowers. The profusion of colors and their gentle movement in the breeze arouse our delight. As we gaze at this sight, another kind of longing stirs us, one not so quickly sated. We linger over this pleasure, and savoring the experience does not diminish our interest. Our mood is not relief but gratitude. We tend to describe this pleasure in the present tense: "How good it is to be here!"

Sexual pleasure encompasses both need and appreciation. Neglecting this complexity, we diminish sexuality and imperil its pleasure. If we focus on sex as instinctual arousal, the goal is speedy relief. As with the thirst on a hot day, genital arousal can be quickly satisfied. The pleasure comes through physical stimulation, not the presence of a lover. But this release leaves us gratified rather than grateful.

The sex drive is a profound biological reality, the basis of our survival as a species. Nevertheless, the need pleasure is enriched in the pleasure of appreciation, the special delight that stirs in the presence of our lover. In a pleasure akin to wonder, we recognize that this is not just someone with whom to have sex. Erotic appreciation makes us eager to explore and embrace every aspect of the person—body, ideas, values, feelings, hopes.

As our appreciation grows, we desire to *give* pleasure to the partner. This pleasuring—in body and in spirit—brings us great joy. When sex involves more than satisfying a biological need, its pleasure leads us into the complex world of partnership. We learn, perhaps only after some initial awkwardness, the different rhythms and moods of sexual pleasuring between us. Honoring these differences, we find that shared pleasure deepens our life together. More at ease in letting go of control of ourselves and of the relationship, we surrender to the pleasure-giving initiative of our partner.

Erotic appreciation invites us to linger in one another's presence. This complex pleasure emboldens us to risk a lifelong commitment and to open ourselves to new life that may be a gift of our love. Learning to receive pleasure as well as to give pleasure comes as the gift of *eros*.

FOR FURTHER REFLECTION

Recall a recent experience of genuine pleasure. Spend some moments bringing this experience to mind, savoring the memory.

Now consider:

> How did this experience of pleasure help to make you *present*?
>
> In what ways did this experience make you *grateful*?
>
> Are there ways in which this experience led you to be more *generous*?
>
> Can you identify a chief obstacle these days to your experience of genuine pleasure?
>
> What can be done to overcome this barrier to pleasure in your life?

PART THREE

UNEXPECTED PATHWAYS TO EROS

The energy of eros moves us toward others
in affection, cooperation, and devoted love.

Hope, with its surprising energy,
serves as another threshold of eros.

Suffering seems an unlikely pathway for eros, but its arousals
—alerting us to our own pain and to the distress of others—
stir us to both resist and endure.

Anger and compassion open further pathways of grace.

9

Eros of Hope

UNINVITED ENVOY FROM ANOTHER WORLD

For in hope we are saved.
Now hope that is seen is not hope.
For who hopes for what is seen?
But if we hope for what we do not see,
we wait for it in patience.
— Romans 8:24–25

Hope is a curious phenomenon, inviting us to expect some-thing good from the future. Hope may come as an enduring mood enlivening us over weeks and months. It often arrives in a sudden surge of energy that enables us, even against the evidence, to believe in something new and something "more." As *eros*, hope prepares us to pursue possibilities that we cannot always account for. Hope comes also as a grace; we can hope even for what we cannot accomplish on our own. In these movements of *eros* and grace, hope opens unexpected pathways to a passionate God.

Roberto Unger describes hope as an ennobling passion, an en-ergy that awakens us to new possibilities and expands our capacity for generous action. For Unger, "hope appears as an uninvited envoy from another world, resolving conflicts that seemed insolu-ble and breaking through frontiers that looked impassable. It has the force of surprise."

An uninvited envoy: As we begin to hope in the midst of a threatening situation, often we do not know the source of this emotion and grace. Hope is a fragile gift, not a sure possession, as it brings visions of tomorrow's possible worlds. Hope catches us by surprise, its erotic force moving us past barriers that, moments before, seemed impregnable. Hope shares the extravagance of *eros*, showing us a grander and richer existence beyond today's mundane world.

Present circumstances and prevailing arrangements in world politics, in the national economy, or in our own families can lock us into socially prescribed behaviors. But, as David Tracy reminds us, "the opposite of hope is neither pessimism nor despair, but apathy." God's words of hope would rouse us from our apathy: "I am about to do a new thing; now it springs forth, do you not perceive it?" (Isa 43:19). Hope's vision sees through the strictures of the status quo, the "received wisdom" that insists the current arrangement—whether in society or in my own life—is how things must be.

Hope can also alter the past. Often we sense that the past is over and finished, that we cannot undo the "spilt milk" of our mistakes. American culture encourages us to put our failings or grief behind us and move on. But the past has not really finished with us. It survives in unhealed wounds, inherited fears, and unquenched desires for revenge. Hope rallies us against such fatalism by giving us, as Unger notes, "the ability to downgrade the influence of past and present structures and compulsions."

In his novel *About Schmidt*, Louis Begley writes: "The past has no imperatives that the present cannot refuse." Hope ennobles us by making it possible to forgive the past, our own immature or destructive actions as well as the offenses of others. Without the capacity for forgiveness that is ignited by the *eros* of hope, the past is indeed finished; we are then doomed to stoic endurance or to endless worry and fantasies of revenge.

The transformative power of hope also shapes the future. The grace of hope allows us to imagine our tomorrows in more generous ways, reassuring us that the future need not be simply "more of the same." Just as it challenges the finality of the past, hope undermines the fatalism of the future.

FALSE HOPES AND HOPEFUL PROMISES

A university student aspires to become a doctor but cannot master the required science courses. Motivation for this career is strong, but the reality of personal skills does not fit the dream. The student's challenge is to explore deeper dimensions of the dream, to find other ways to bring healing into the world. Here hope may spark imagination and courage to help reconstruct the dream.

Another person approaches death after a long battle with cancer. In some settings physician, chaplain, and family members will conspire to offer reassurance, leading the patient to anticipate improvement. This unrealistic expectation may deprive the dying person of the opportunity to grieve, to revisit and reconcile with the past, to say goodbye to family and friends. Here false hope has blocked the path to a deeper meaning.

The virtue of hope emerges from the potential carried in our promises. Our promises thrust us into a future we have not yet seen and cannot control. We pledge ourselves to persons and to values, based only on what we know now. This may seem irrational, but we quickly learn that there is no other way. And in the process of living, we are consoled to find that we can keep our promises. Without such promises, made and kept, our lives bear no fruit.

Promise, the peculiar force that binds the present to an unseen future, lies at the heart of the Jewish and Christian relationship with God. In the Bible God makes promises—of rescue from slavery in Egypt, of "land flowing with milk and honey," of return from exile, of the future reign of justice and peace. It is hope that enables us to embrace these promises, drawing us beyond what our own efforts can achieve.

Early in life we may think of hope as a mood of optimism, a sense of confidence. Only later, as the disciplines of maturity have their purifying effect, do we recognize that hope is different. Optimism is rooted in confidence that we will be successful; it is grounded in a sense of personal strength and competence. Aware of our own skills, and backed by stout allies and good companions, how can we fail? Through our middle years, this optimism is likely to be bruised as we encounter the inflexible forces of society and the limits of our own abilities.

If we are fortunate, as optimism gives way to a more sober judgment about reality, our hope will survive. Recognizing that our hope is not anchored in our own strengths, we honor it both as gift and as grace. On our dark days, we are tempted to despair of the integrity of politicians, the vision of church leaders, or the capacity of our economic system to address the disparity between rich and poor. Yet still we hope. Despite all evidence to the contrary, we hold to the belief that life can be other than it is. Like Paul, we hope against hope. Our confidence now arises from the conviction that God will prevail.

Paul Ricoeur traces the transformation of *eros* as hope emerges from the despair of reason. In much of life, we rely on the clarifying power of analytic reason to guide us. But at critical junctures this power reaches its limit. Critical thinking alone cannot explain life's ultimate meaning, or fathom the human capacity for sacrifice, or justify our yearning for eternal life. In the face of these enduring mysteries, Ricoeur concludes, "reason must first despair." Despair, however, brings not disaster, but an opening to something new: "This reaching of a limit of reason and its despair is the beginning of hope.... Hope opens up what knowledge claims to close."

MEDICAL PERSPECTIVES ON HOPE

In *The Anatomy of Hope*, physician Jerome Groopman explores the impact of hope on illness and recovery. He begins by identifying hope as "the elevating feeling we experience when we see—in the mind's eye—a path to a better future." Physicians and hospital chaplains have long been aware of a correlation between hope and health. As hope diminishes, a patient's immune system is compromised. But a patient blessed by hope may well face illness, and even death, with uncommon resourcefulness.

Medical researchers are aware of the workings of the placebo effect: When a patient is cared for by an attentive caregiver, the body releases hormones that facilitate healing—even when the "medicine" administered is actually a safe but inert compound. Groopman comments that while the placebo drug is inactive, the patient's mind is not.

When organs are diseased and the body's systems are failing, nerve receptors send pain signals to the brain, signals "that potently amplify our feelings of fear, anxiety, and despair." This development can become a vicious cycle: "When we feel pain from our physical debility," Groopman continues, "that pain amplifies our sense of hopelessness; the less hopeful we feel, the fewer endorphins . . . we release." This cycle can be broken by the first spark of hope: "Emotions like hope can also release endorphins that block the 'on' cells so that the pain signals are not sent to the brain." Groopman adds, "Hope sets off a chain reaction. Hope tempers pain, and as we sense less pain, that feeling of hope expands, which further reduces pain."

Another physician-author, Abraham Verghese, warns us of the negative impact of a culturally imposed optimism. He notes that "modern society sometimes counters old-fashioned fatalism surrounding the word 'cancer' by embracing the idea that our wills possess nearly supernatural powers." The implication seems to be that what brings us down is not the disease, but a temperamental deficiency or weakness of will. As a result, patients sometimes feel they must exhibit a hopeful stance, regardless of the physical symptoms or emotional responses they may be experiencing. Verghese notes that "many patients feel they must be optimistic; they are pressured to deny those moments when they are dispirited or pessimistic. These feelings, society implies, are shameful and will cost you the battle." Groopman identifies this kind of optimism as false hope. Genuine hope includes the capacity to acknowledge both the genuine threat and "a path to a better future."

THE PATIENCE OF HOPE

"If we hope for what we do not see, we wait for it in patience" (Rom 8:25). Even in the post–9/11 world, Americans tend to be optimistic people. Citizens in a still-youthful nation that has suffered few calamities, we feel kindly toward history and confident that we can shape our own destiny (and perhaps that of the world).

We are a hopeful nation but an impatient people. In a land of multi-tasking and rising productivity, surrounded by promises of instant gratification, we do not endure waiting well. Among many Americans, patience has a bad reputation. Identified with the humble submission expected of women and the poor in their assigned social roles, patience seems a weakness, too passive, insufficiently assertive. Poet Adrienne Rich infuses vigor into this un-American virtue. In her poem "A Wild Patience Has Taken Me This Far" she describes the force that has guided her through protest and crisis. In her struggle to integrate the once-conflicting energies of anger and tenderness, a rough-hewn patience has sustained her. For the poet, this wild patience has led her to life in abundance.

The virtue of patience fuses hope with courage. What we hope for often requires of us patience—as well as great courage. Thomas Aquinas observed that the original understanding of courage was linked to "manliness." Courage and fortitude were associated with the muscular strength that warriors display in a willingness to face injury and death. But Aquinas argued that a deeper appreciation of courage moves beyond this combative orientation to a broader range of endurance. He linked courage with patience, noting that courage frequently demands a firm resolve, a commitment to pursue important values despite threat and danger. Aquinas recognized sadness and grief as unavoidable in the face of life's many disappointments; these emotions can spiral down into melancholy and depression. Patience protects us from this dangerous descent. Patience permits people to be properly saddened by all the troubles to be faced, yet not so overcome that they abandon their valuable contributions to this wounded world.

From this perspective, patience is not at all passive. Arming us with endurance, patience allows us to live in a way that is fully alert. Aquinas testifies, in one commentator's words, that "patience keeps us from the danger that our spirit may be broken by grief and lose its greatness." Patience is a crucial element of what psychologists identify as "receptive mastery," the ability to bear what life offers us without being defeated by it.

Courage and patience are both rooted in hope—the expectation that safety is close at hand. This expectation is anchored not in our own abilities but in the belief that God will prevail. Such confidence allows us to acknowledge the risks we face in pursuing significant values, even as we affirm that the risks are worthwhile. Patience lifts us out of our narrow self-concern and centers our attention on God's future. The erotic power of hope is an exercise in courage, defended by the endurance of patience.

HOPE IN THE REIGN OF GOD

"The reign of God is at hand"; thus begins Jesus' ministry in Mark's gospel. At the start of his public life, Jesus set out a stunning vision: a world transformed by love and justice. In Jesus' energetic hope, this reality was already breaking into the world. When asked the location of this kingdom, Jesus answered, "The reign of God is among you" (Lk 17:21; authors' translation). The reign of God exists first in hope-filled imaginations. But Jesus proclaimed that God's kingdom comes—is actualized among us—in acts of mercy and justice. In every gesture of compassion, the reign of God moves toward social reality; in every act of violence and greed, this sacred dream retreats, seeming like mere illusion. In the face of chronic injustice, hope in the reign of God becomes increasingly difficult to sustain.

Hope in God's reign envisions a life that is at once "much more" and "not yet." Theologian Jürgen Moltmann describes this tension: God's promise of new life "calls this world into question— not because to the eye of hope it is as nothing, but because to the eye of hope it is not yet what it has the prospect of being." Genuine Christian hope is directed to a future that is both distant and at hand. A future that is too distant begets escape into fantasyland or "pie in the sky when we die." It is not tethered to our own acts of generosity and justice. A hoped-for future that too much reflects the present situation quickly becomes identified with a current regime or dominant economic system. The risk here is that a particular political agenda will substitute for the kingdom of God.

The kingdom of God expresses a paradox of hope. It is a vision that lies within the range of our imagination; we recognize that our own actions of care and concern influence its realization. At the same time, God's reign lies utterly beyond us. We can envision what we cannot achieve; we aspire to what we ourselves cannot bring about. This poignant truth is not a design flaw in our nature, but a characteristic of our humanity—as both finite and created for life with God.

SPECIAL CELEBRATIONS OF HOPE

Weddings are hopeful celebrations, even in the face of rising divorce rates. The birth of a baby announces to all—not just the parents—that new possibilities lie ahead. Graduation ceremonies carry a message of hope as well.

We end this chapter with a reflection delivered at a recent graduation ceremony at Catholic Theological Union in Chicago.

> Graduations are hopeful occasions—as you finish the mini-marathon of your program, you are hopeful that there will be a place for you to make a contribution, to make a difference. You hope that all the tuition you expended has not been wasted, that there is a job out there for you. This is a hopeful occasion.
>
> You bring your learning and gifts to a world in which hope is in short supply and hard to come by. For many, hope has been diminished by our nation's bold but disastrous experiments on the international scene. For many, hope has been jeopardized by recent scandals and malpractice in the church. We have too many friends and colleagues—mature, holy people—whose hope no longer runs through the religious institution where they were long nourished. They have taken their hopes elsewhere.

Perhaps this depletion of hope makes sense in a time like ours. If our emotions are meant to tune us to the world, we should feel some of the disappointment that churns through our society. To put it more starkly: With all that is taking place in our land and our church these days, if you are not depressed once in a while, your medication is too strong. You might want to dial it back a bit so you can experience what the rest of us are feeling.

When philosopher Roberto Unger defines hope as "an uninvited envoy from another world," he is expressing in post-modern prose a pre-modern insight about the giftedness and gracefulness of hope. We cannot summon it, manufacture it, or guarantee it.

If hope is an envoy from another world, it arrives by way of real people and earthly institutions. God's grace is not magical, but incarnational; hope touches us by way of other fragile lives and faulty human organizations. If we cannot generate or guarantee our hope, we can still foster it. We do that by remaining close to hopeful people, hopeful texts such as the Bible, and hopeful communities.

FOR FURTHER REFLECTION

In a mood of quiet, bring to mind a personal experience of genuine hope—a time or season when the future appeared full of promise.

Take time to savor this experience of hope: What possibilities did it announce? What obstacles or barriers did it challenge?

In your experience, what can be done to nurture and strengthen hope—in personal life, in faith communities, in our civic life?

10

Eros of Suffering

ENERGY TO RESIST AND TO ACCEPT

I have observed the misery of my people...
I know their sufferings, and I have come down to deliver them
from the Egyptians...
— Exodus 3:7–8

E*ros* expands our life; suffering diminishes it. *Eros* opens pathways to joy and delight; suffering leads down avenues of sorrow and anxiety. What could *eros* and suffering possibly have in common?

Suffering arouses us—at least to our own pain. Pain gets our attention; it is an alarm that makes us mindful of our embodied selves. When pain signals harm, *eros* comes as energy to respond. *Eros* is also aroused in compassion for the suffering of others. Both our own distress and another person's misery engage us in the passion of life. Suffering is both a problem to solve (how to eradicate needless suffering?) and a mystery to be savored (what is the meaning of unavoidable suffering?).

TWO ICONS OF SUFFERING

In hundreds of thousands of statues, gigantic and miniature, the Buddha sits in repose. His hands rest peacefully on crossed legs. The face of the Enlightened One radiates calm. All suffering has vanished. Having let go of grasping and anxiety, the Buddha displays the ideal of transcending all disturbance and suffering.

Jesus hangs on a wretched cross, his body twisted in pain as blood drains from multiple wounds. In this sacred icon the suffering, so raw and deep, seems to be the point. Paradox abounds here: an innocent person is dramatically tortured in public, but this suffering holds the promise of transforming and transcending evil and loss.

The icon of the Buddha announces eloquently that suffering is largely our own doing; we bring it upon ourselves. Our wants and cravings, our lusts and fears, fuel our endless anxieties. Buddhists remind us there are ways to rid ourselves of this unnecessary distress. Quieting our acquisitive habits, we can abandon the illusion that each of us is a separate "self" destined always to compete with others. Following these disciplines, we can come into an enlightened stillness (nirvana) in which suffering has been vanquished. Buddha's message is that—ultimately—suffering is not real.

The life of Jesus tells a different story, one in which suffering is most real. Suffering cannot be evaded, since loss and sorrow are embedded in the script of human life. As we link our lives with others, persons who are mortal like ourselves, we are certain to suffer. If we love at all, we will surely come to grief.

The Buddhist and Christian paths converge in compassion, beckoning us to enter into the suffering of others. If we commit to the works of compassion, we are certain to be felled repeatedly by the injustice that stalks the world. As part of the human drama, suffering is more than simply evil. Though pervasive and destructive, suffering also plays a mysterious role in the alchemy of human maturing and spiritual growth.

Both of these religious traditions reveal the truth. Human suffering often springs from our own clinging and anxiety. Violence toward others and abuse of ourselves account for much of the world's distress. Worry over what we already possess and fear about what we may lose generate a major portion of the world's pain.

And yet . . . human folly does not account for all the suffering in the world. Mortals live in fragile environments, where we are prone to accidents, illness, and other catastrophes both temporary and terminal. Despite the advances of modern medicine, with its antibiotics, anesthetics, and surgery, limits still loom. Bodies age, nerves fray, and humans move inevitably toward their demise—a progress often accompanied by pain.

Religions have long struggled to distinguish self-generated suffering from the mysteries of our fragile mortality. For which sorrows are we culpable? Perhaps we can learn to avoid these. But what of suffering that defies all explanation? Here another response is demanded. Social scientist Clifford Geertz, a lifelong student of religion, judges that the problem "is not how to avoid suffering, but how to suffer, how to make of physical pain, personal loss, worldly defeat, or the helpless contemplation of others' agony something bearable, supportable."

MAKING SENSE OF SUFFERING

Suffering may be too general a term to cover the range of human distress—from the horror of physical torture to the chronic ache of migraine headaches; from the loss of a child to cancer to our willingness to sacrifice our life for a person we love. Still, in every age and culture humans have tried to make sense of the scandal of suffering. In ancient China, for example, the philosopher Mencius observed:

> Heaven, when it is about to place a great burden on a person, always first tests his resolution, exhausts his frame and makes him suffer starvation and hardship, frustrates his efforts so as to shake him from his mental lassitude, toughen his nature and make good his deficiencies.

According to Mencius, suffering readies us for our vocation. In the moral universe that he envisions, suffering comes as a discipline to test and toughen a person in preparation for a challenging career. Paul also recognized a connection between suffering and personal destiny: "We also boast in our sufferings, knowing that suffering produces endurance and endurance produces character and character produces hope" (Rom 5:3–4).

Two millennia later, Karl Marx explored the link between suffering and religion: "Religious suffering is at the same time the expression of a real suffering and also a protest against real suffering." For the atheist Marx, even religious suffering, as a signal of the world's troubles, was genuine. Part of suffering's purpose is to alert us to injustice.

Artists, too, have been fascinated by human suffering. The ancient Greeks took up this question in great dramatic performances. Classic Greek works portray the suffering of both gods and humans caught up in intricate plots of betrayal, loss, and grief. In *Prometheus Bound*, the playwright Aeschylus recounts the myth of the god who gave to humans the divine gift of fire. For this act, the other gods sentenced Prometheus to be eternally chained to a rock at the edge of the world. In spite of his suffering, Prometheus did not repent. He accepted pain and disgrace as the price to be paid for his heroic action. The lesson here: Suffering may accompany heroic deeds.

The Greek dramatist Sophocles tells the tragic story of Antigone. Faced with an impossible choice between obedience to the king and piety toward her dead brother, Antigone chose a fate filled with suffering. This noble woman determined to bury her dead brother despite the king's warning that doing so would bring about her death. In her integrity, she could find no alternative. Antigone did not repent of her decision; she would honor her brother, embracing the death her courageous act would bring.

These classics present the reality of human suffering in a dramatic form that leads to *catharsis*—a cleansing that enables the audience to come to terms with suffering and tragedy in their own lives. Like the authors of the Bible, the classic dramatists sensed that suffering was somehow a necessary part of the plot. Contemporary director David Mamet discusses the healing effect of great drama on the imagination: When we watch a well-crafted play, he says, "we have, through following the course of the drama, left aside . . . the delusion that we are powerful and wise, and we leave the theater better for the rest." Martha Nussbaum has called this cleansing effect "healing without cure."

DOES SUFFERING COME AS PUNISHMENT?

As humans have struggled to understand the meaning of suffering, many have focused on its function as punishment. When a person who habitually mistreats others is finally brought to justice, we feel satisfied: "He got what he deserved." A woman who habitually takes risks that put her health in danger dies an early death; again, we can make sense of this—"She brought it on herself." The ancient belief in *karma* follows a similar line of reasoning: A person's present joy or current distress can be traced to previous actions, either in this lifetime or in an earlier one.

If the universe is moral, so that people receive what they deserve, we can make sense of suffering. But, of course, people do not always get what they deserve. Evildoers are known to prosper, and none of us has received the full measure of what we are due. We have been gifted and favored with benefits for which we cannot account; we have been forgiven beyond our merits. The moral accounting of good and evil does not come out even; there remains the puzzle of suffering that is not obviously tethered to moral wrong, just as we are blessed beyond our deserving.

For Jews and Christians, the search for the meaning of suffering begins in the first book of the Bible. In Genesis, we read of the consequences of Adam and Eve's turning away from their gracious Creator: "To the woman God said: 'I will greatly increase your pangs in childbearing; in pain you shall bring forth children" (Gen 3:16). To Adam God said, "Cursed is the ground because of you; in toil you shall eat of it all the days of your life; thorns and thistles it shall bring forth for you. . . . By the sweat of your face you shall eat bread until you return to the ground out of which you were taken" (Gen 3:17–19). In Genesis, the physical pain associated with childbirth and the onerous struggle for daily sustenance are linked with moral fault; our sinfulness accounts for our suffering.

In the New Testament, this association of suffering with sin continues. For Paul, death is not the natural end to a mortal life, but capital punishment for sin. "The wages of sin is death" (Rom 6:23). The message is clearly that we have brought our suffering upon ourselves. Paul Ricoeur sums up this broad conviction of the ancient world that we are the sources of our suffering: "If you suffer, if you are ill, if you fail, if you die, it is because you have sinned." Any human disorder—whether physical or mental—and any disruption in nature—such as a drought or flood—was seen as an indictment that humans had done something wrong. For many centuries, this was the best wisdom about suffering.

In the Hebrew Scriptures, one man raised new and disturbing questions about suffering. The story of Job tells us about a wealthy and pious man with a large family and many possessions. Suddenly, he is struck by significant troubles: crop failure, the death of family members, extensive personal ailments. As his suffering accumulates, Job struggles to understand this sudden change of events. What has he done to deserve this?

Unable to explain his torments, Job curses the day he was born. Well-meaning friends offer consolation and urge him to acknowledge his own evil deeds as the cause of his suffering. Job's children come under the same judgment: "Your children must have been evil: God has punished them for their crimes" (Job 8:4). Again, the conventional wisdom about a moral universe prevails here: suffering can arise only from sin.

Refusing to accept this account, Job turns to God in bitter lament, demanding to know the cause of his suffering. But God refuses to offer Job an explanation for his distress. Instead, God appears dramatically—"out of a whirlwind"—to challenge Job's audacity: "Where were you when I laid the foundations of the earth?...Have you commanded the morning since your days began, or caused the dawn to know its place?" (Job 38:4, 12). Job is reduced to silence. "I have uttered what I did not understand, things too wonderful for me, which I did not know...therefore I despise myself, and repent in dust and ashes" (Job 42:3, 6).

Later editors of this biblical story found its implications shocking and added an epilogue (Job 42:7–17) in which Job is suddenly restored to full health and prosperity. This ending reverts to the comfort of a well-balanced moral universe: Job's suffering was only a trial from God. Job passed the test and so, once again, all is well. Such an ending, of course, contradicts the more mysterious theme at the heart of this biblical text.

The unsettling core of Job's story is that not all suffering is punishment. Moral wrongdoing does not fully explain the mystery of human distress. Later in the Bible, Jesus reinforces this separation of suffering from sin. Jesus' followers bring him a man born blind and ask the cause of his disability: "Who sinned, this man or his parents, that he was born blind?" (Jn 9:2). Their assumption is that a physical disability must arise from a moral fault. But Jesus responds, "Neither this man nor his parents sinned."

SUFFERING—SAYING "NO"

Suffering is both a challenge to be confronted and a mystery to be embraced. Much human suffering—the very stuff of our vulnerability and mortality—remains a mystery. But much of the pain and distress that assaults us, as Buddha recognized, is our own doing. To this latter suffering, we must dare to say "no."

A great deal of the suffering in our world is man-made. Echoing Buddha's insight, philosopher Martha Nussbaum emphasizes that the bulk of humanity's pain and suffering does not "result from the very structure of human life, or from some mysterious necessity of nature. It results from ignorance, greed, malice, and various other forms of badness." She concludes, "Many conflicts that at first seem intractable can . . . be surmounted with intelligent planning."

Contemporary theologians, too, urge us to move beyond abstract speculation about the origins of evil toward a shared search for strategies to relieve suffering. Saying "no" to suffering begins with the recognition of *negative contrast experiences*. Edward Schillebeeckx uses this term to name "those experiences of injustice, oppression, and suffering that give rise to protest and the ethical imperative toward active transformation." Theologian Catherine Hilkert adds: "In the indignation, lament, and active resistance to which these 'negative contrast experiences' give rise, the eyes of faith can detect the power of the Spirit of God at work on behalf of the future of humankind and the cosmos." Negative contrast experiences engender the *eros* of anger rising up against injustice and the *eros* of hope for something better. Here the energy of *eros* moves us toward resistance.

The cry of those who suffer is the first call to social change; their pain alerts us that "this cannot go on." In ancient Egypt, God heard the cry of the Hebrew slaves. "I have observed the misery of my people who are in Egypt; I have heard their cry on account of their taskmasters. Indeed, I know their sufferings, and I have come down to deliver them from the Egyptians..." (Ex 3:7–8). For our religious ancestors, prophecy began in the visceral recognition that things were not right, and continued in the indictment of social wrongs.

Saying "no" to suffering happens in many ways. On the personal level, medical caregivers today give increased attention to managing the pain and physical distress of their patients, even when a cure is unlikely. On the social level, expanded awareness of poverty and discrimination motivates citizens to do something about these evils by addressing their underlying causes in the structures of society. Compassion for unnecessary suffering moves people to take practical action in order to transform unjust systems. And globally, worldwide relief efforts—Doctors Without Borders, Amnesty International, Catholic Relief Services, and others—continue to say "no" to the world's suffering.

SUFFERING—SAYING "YES"

Despite dramatic advances in science and philanthropy, much suffering remains—perhaps never to be fully vanquished. Psychologist Erik Erikson sounds the sober reminder: "Life eventually makes patients of us all." Whatever our technological or psychological advances, we continue to face suffering. Unavoidable distress is humanity's plight, lying beyond the scope of our tools of healing and emancipation.

In her extraordinary book, *After Such Knowledge*, Eva Hoffman reflects on the ways in which the suffering her parents endured in the Holocaust was handed on to her. Coming to America after having lost most of their extended family during this tragedy, her parents brought with them a deep reservoir of traumatic grief. Their pain, unwittingly handed on to their daughter, was not bound in conscious memory of losses they had mourned. "The legacy they passed on was not a processed, mastered past, but the splintered signs of acute suffering, of grief and loss."

Hoffman mourns her parents' unresolved losses, now haunting her own life. Her effort is to name these sufferings, bring them to the light of consciousness, and thus release herself from their power over her. Her goal is to acknowledge the unnamed sufferings, saying "yes" to them in a way that will exorcise their destructive power.

How is such unbearable suffering transformed? Hoffman's tentative answer is that "suffering shared, suffering respected, is suffering endurable." Honoring the pain begins in the archeological effort of bringing buried grief to light.

Hoffman distinguishes between two kinds of suffering: trauma and tragedy. "Tragic struggle," she says, "may entail moral agony, but it leaves the sense of identity and dignity intact." Thus, the suffering of Antigone, Job, and Jesus would qualify as tragedy. Traumatic suffering implodes in life-shattering grief. Trauma, Hoffman suggests, "is suffering in excess of what the psyche can absorb, a suffering that twists the soul until it can no longer straighten itself out, and so piercingly sharp that it fragments the wholeness of the self." *Fragments* and *splinters* are key images in Hoffman's analysis. Trauma tears away a person's identity, leaving dignity in shreds.

Traumatic suffering is passed on to the next generation, but the transmission travels underground and out of sight. Hoffman describes the child's reception of a parent's pain as "transferred loss." Since the parents' distress is not consciously absorbed, there is no acknowledgment. And without acknowledgment no healing can begin. As a child Hoffman did not experience the traumatic events of her parents' lives directly, but she suffered the unconscious aftermath of their losses—expressed in her parents' anxieties, melancholic silence, and unexplained anger. The unconscious transmission of such trauma leads, Hoffman asserts, to "impossible attachments, impossible enmeshments."

Chinese scholar Ci Jiwei, reflecting on the bitter fruit of the Cultural Revolution in his own country, offers similar judgment. Because the trauma endured in that decade cannot publicly be acknowledged, the distress has "sedimented in the body as lack of vigor and sedimented in the mind as cynicism." People may try to forget the horrors of their past sufferings, but their bodies remember; grief denied descends into the body, biding its time and resurfacing in the guise of other symptoms. For this scholar, as for Hoffman, "recollection brings hidden memories into consciousness; no longer hidden or incapacitated by them, we can afford the luxury of remembering." In this delayed remembering, we may at last say "yes" to suffering.

Dietrich Bonhoeffer, a Christian theologian martyred by the Nazis, struggled to make sense of suffering in his life. He refused the Christian temptation to turn it into a piety of pain. "Suffering is never an absolute; it is not an end in itself or even a higher state of godliness than blessing. Both suffering and blessing are fruits of setting ourselves entirely at God's disposal."

The *eros* of suffering arouses us to ethical action to alleviate needless pain. On this pathway, *eros* engages us in the transformation of an unjust world. The *eros* of suffering also awakens in us a mystical recognition that God's compassion will triumph over all; this pathway of *eros* moves us to stand in solidarity with those who suffer now.

For Further Reflection

In a mood of calm and peace, consider the wisdom gained from your experience of suffering—both your own anguish and other people's distress. Take care in this reflection, since remembered suffering easily reawakens our pain.

Drawing on these memories, identify the responses—attitudes or actions, virtues or strategies—that helped you to say "no," to resist the suffering arising from human malice and injustice. In your experience, what is the role of courage and patience in response to suffering?

Then identify the responses—attitudes or actions, virtues or strategies—that have helped you to say "yes," acknowledging the mystery of suffering that defies explanation. In your experience, what is the role of grief and lament in response to suffering?

11

Eros of Anger

RESOURCE FOR SOCIAL TRANSFORMATION

Then Jesus entered the temple
and drove out all who were selling and buying in the temple,
and he overturned the tables of the money changers,
and the seats of those who sold doves.
— Matthew 21:12

The *eros* of anger is the energy of social transformation. Anger arises in the service of life; it is the passion—painful but crucial—that energizes our commitments and sustains our resolve in the face of injustice.

Such a view of anger sits uneasily with a religious tradition that favors the image of Jesus as "meek and humble of heart." Does not anger rank high in the traditional list of seven deadly sins? Yet in the midst of this enduring prejudice against anger, we recall other biblical testimony. The prophet Jeremiah raged at his community's unjust behaviors: "I am full of the wrath of the Lord and I am weary of holding it in" (Jer 6:11).

Such holy anger is not restricted to the Hebrew Scriptures. Throughout the gospel we again and again meet an angry Jesus. Not only does he overturn the tables of those trading in front of the temple, he frequently lashes out at the pseudo-righteous: "Woe to you, scribes and Pharisees, hypocrites!" (Mt 23:13). When Peter counsels him not to risk a return trip to Jerusalem, Jesus' anger flashes again: "Get behind me, Satan!" (Mt 16:23).

And when confronted by people who would prevent him from healing the sick on the sabbath, Jesus "looked around at them in anger" (Mk 3:5). In the lives of the Old Testament prophets and in the life of Jesus, anger was an honorable emotion.

The Christian vocation calls us to continue Jesus' ministry in our own lives. In our works of love, anger is not simply a misadventure or a sign of moral weakness. Anger can be an essential resource for facing injustice. It is the passion that equips us to challenge wrongdoers and to stand up to malice in the world.

Most of us are familiar with anger's ambiguous effects. Sometimes the honest expression of anger can move a relationship to a deeper level of trust; in other circumstances, anger can end a friendship. We know that anger plays an important role in social reform; we know equally well that anger stands behinds much of the violence that plagues contemporary society.

These mixed experiences leave us uneasy. We dislike feeling anger, with its visceral arousal and mental distress. And we fear the consequences of anger in hostility unleashed or relationships destroyed. But even as we count anger's costs, we recognize more than liability. Anger is sometimes an ally that protects us from harm, reminds us of our values, and energizes us to act.

Anger intensifies our connection with the world, alerting us to possible threats and arming us for action. Granted, it is easy to subvert this passion, divert its energy, or misconstrue its protective purposes. But befriended, anger is a valued companion. Anger is always assertive, as it makes its claim and indicts injustice. But anger is not always aggressive. The *eros* of anger moves us, but the goal of our anger need not include inflicting harm on other people.

In everyday contacts, the demands of our complex lifestyles often leave us ready to be angry. An inconsiderate passenger pushes ahead of us on a crowded bus; a rude sales agent ignores our request for assistance; an all-night party in the neighborhood interrupts our sleep; a last-minute demand at work keeps us from making it home before rush-hour traffic begins. We all need better ways of handling stress. Sometimes the remedy is to simplify our daily schedule so that we feel less under siege. More often, we learn to turn away from these routine provocations and get on with our lives.

Anger also flares in the face of genuine grievance. We see people we love treated unfairly; a colleague's behavior offends our sense of decency or fair play; a politician shows contempt for values that are at the core of our worldview. When we are confronted by injury or injustice, the *eros* of anger fuels our commitment to right the wrong. All of us can recognize ways in which this would-be righteous anger can misfire, provoking behaviors that are self-destructive or target the wrong enemy. But anger aroused by injustice plays an indispensable role in social life. Theologian Beverly Harrison reminds us: "We must never lose touch with the fact that all serious moral activity, especially action for social change, takes its bearing from the rising power of human anger."

The philosopher Aristotle was among the first to recognize the positive potential of anger. Three and a half centuries before the Common Era, he introduced the metaphor of "temper" into his discussion of emotions. The metal meant to be used in a new sword must be tempered, so that it becomes strong and flexible— neither too brittle not too pliant. So too, good-tempered persons are not too easily aroused. And, once aroused, they are more likely to find appropriate expression of their strong emotions.

Aristotle emphasized the need both to experience and to express anger. "Those who are not angry at the things they should be angry at are thought to be fools." These people, unable to defend themselves or to challenge injustice around them, are ill-tempered in a special sense. They have "lost their temper," not in rage but in stoic passivity. According to Aristotle, we abuse anger as an essential human capacity not only in senseless displays of violence but also in the inability to be aroused when circumstances call for our response.

Thomas Aquinas, who translated Aristotle's civic responsibilities into Christian virtues, highlighted the complexity of anger. Anger often comes with sadness (about an injury or injustice sustained) and also with hope (that we might correct a negative situation). The angry person, Aquinas noted, seeks vindication, but the Latin word he used—*vindicta*—can mean either "vindication" or "vengeance." If anger necessarily moves us toward revenge, then clearly it has no place among the Christian virtues. But Thomas insisted on the positive potential of anger. Purified through the discipline of discernment and placed at the service of justice and love, anger becomes a virtue. Tempered, the *eros* of anger fuels courage and commitment.

ANGER AND JUSTICE

Anger makes a moral claim: A wrong has been done and it must be set right. In response to injustice, anger moves us to remedy an intolerable situation. Sometimes expressing anger is enough, and just letting people know of our distress brings about the needed change. Most often, the world does not come around so quickly in the face of our displeasure. Systemic injustice seldom yields to short-term solutions. When our goal is social change, we must do more than register our distress; we must work to make things different. Here strategies of planning and problem-solving are crucial; we must be clear about what we want to accomplish, recognize the barriers we face, gather needed resources, and enlist allies. But we may be reluctant to embrace the emotion of anger since, as Dana Crowley Jack observes, "anger potentially brings a clarity of vision and a requirement to act that threatens the established order."

When we confront wrongdoing, anger gives us steam that makes things happen, but being steamed up does not guarantee success. Justice is seldom served by the hot urgency of rage. The heat of anger burns us out, and sometimes leads us to act against our own best judgments. Outbursts of rage just make matters worse. Channeling anger into effective action is the real work of change. Justice anger, when carefully cultivated, helps to sustain us through the lengthy processes of clarifying goals, developing a plan of action, overcoming obstacles, and celebrating even modest gains.

Acting *with* anger means holding our anger in a new way. Rather than moving away from our arousal, we want to stay in touch with our passion. When we are faced with entrenched bias or long-term patterns of abuse, change can seem impossible. Falling back into a resigned stance that "nothing can be done" or "it's not my job to make things better" is tempting. Resistance seems worthless, but giving in to this sense of futility will sap our strength. If we lose touch with our anger, we will fall out of the loop of social transformation. Conversely, we become equally impotent if we are consumed by our anger and lose the detachment and insight that allow us to use anger's energy as an appropriate tool.

Anger's dangerous memory commits us to action. When apathy threatens, discipline keeps our anger alive. By holding the injustice we have witnessed in mind, recalling injuries we have received, and remembering the values at stake, we rouse ourselves to appropriate response. We honor our anger and transform *eros* into effective action.

But sustaining anger on our own is risky. Remembering anger rekindles emotional pain, and that alone is enough to make us reluctant to stir anger's ashes. We feel that perhaps it is better to turn away from the evidence of personal malice or social inequity and get by as best we can. Finding the support that will help us cope with our emotions is thus an important discipline of anger. With companions who can share in our anger or to whom we can look for support, we gain a sense of power beyond anything that we can do alone. By providing a setting in which our distress is acknowledged and can be focused into action, a supportive group also protects us from simply being overwhelmed by the arousal we feel. The group helps us to hold our pain so that we can draw on its energy for action.

This resilient pursuit of justice requires the right kind of anger and the right kind of community. We need places where the *eros* of anger can be purified and used to forge an effective response. Supportive gatherings—a ministry task force, a small faith community, a network of colleagues, a group of friends—protect us from succumbing to frustration or a desire for revenge. In the safety of these settings, volatile emotions can be acknowledged, confronted, questioned, purified, and confirmed. The goal is seldom to banish anger; we want to moderate our passion but to keep its energy at hand.

Still, anger remains an unpleasant and volatile emotion. Because it threatens our self-control and overturns our serenity, many of us would much prefer to live without it. But the *eros* of anger comes as a necessary disturbance. When we are belittled, when our values are threatened, when injustice imperils our shared life, we must be aroused against these offenses. Befriended and tamed, anger becomes a powerful ally that can help us live responsible lives in our world.

ANGER IN CLOSE RELATIONSHIPS

We have been focusing on the *eros* of anger as the energy of social transformation. Anger is also at play in more personal settings—among families and friends, with co-workers and neighbors. And how we handle our anger has a large impact on these relationships.

In close relationships, expressing anger is sometimes necessary. But contrary to the commonsense advice to "let it all out," the expression of personal outrage does little to dissipate our own or another person's anger. Anger dissolves when the problem between us is recognized and mutual respect is restored. So, learning to express anger appropriately is a valuable skill. Our first impulse may be to throw out an insult to punish the offender. Or, in our hurt, we may want to withdraw our affection and retreat into stony silence or refuse to cooperate. But in close relationships, our goal is usually to move beyond anger toward negotiation, understanding, and peace. If our goal is to make things better, we may wisely conclude that punishment will not heal the situation. Instead, we offer a conciliatory gesture or initiate a problem-solving conversation.

Often "talking it through" is useful, especially when discussion clarifies the situation and strengthens the bonds between us. I can let another person know that I am feeling angry—and why—without attacking that person either verbally or physically. Telling my partner of my distress and how his or her actions have contributed to it is not necessarily hostile behavior. But the way we communicate our anger will significantly shape the results of our conversation.

Sometimes, giving voice to angry feelings moves me beyond apathy ("there is nothing I can do") and self-doubt ("I am probably just getting what I deserve") toward a sense of personal worth and power. But when our goal is to dissipate anger, different skills are required. We experience anger in both mind and body, and both mind and body can be used to dispel its force. We can focus on our state of physical arousal, and counteract anger's "fight or flight" response. Yoga, meditation, and biofeedback exercises influence the autonomic nervous system and lower our physiological arousal. Moderate physical exercise channels energy away from angry behavior. Involving ourselves in an activity we enjoy, especially something that demands our concentration, helps to bring our bodies around in ways that can change our emotional state as well.

Other strategies for moderating anger focus on the judgments we make. Looking at the situation from a wider perspective often helps. Our anger at being kept waiting dissolves when we realize that our companion had a compelling reason for being late. We may excuse an apparent insult when we recognize the strain under which the other person is living. As we become aware of new facts or extenuating circumstances, anger diminishes. Humor too helps us move beyond anger. Being able to laugh at ourselves lessens the impact of the frustrating reversals that are inevitably part of life.

FORGIVENESS IN ANGER

In close relationships, then, resolving anger usually requires an interactive approach. We must acknowledge our mutual distress by facing the troubling issues that confront us, then work together toward practical solutions that we can both live with. Often, we must learn to forgive.

Genuine forgiveness is the fruit of anger courageously faced and resolved. In forgiving, we choose not to let the hurt we have experienced get in the way of a continuing relationship. Forgiveness enables us to start again, to come to a sense of a new beginning. The commonsense adage is to "forgive and forget," but forgiving is not the same as forgetting. In forgiveness, we know that we have sustained hurt, but we respond to others in terms of who they are rather than on the basis of the harm they have inflicted. The order of the adage is important—forgive . . . and then let go the pain, lest its memory revive the anger and hostility between us.

Forgiveness entails a decision that is not completed in the moment of choice. As a process, forgiveness gradually allows the hurt to heal and trust to be restored between us. This process of forgiving does not bring us back to where we were, nor does it allow us to go on as though nothing had happened. Something profound *has* happened, and the fabric of our interwoven lives has been torn. We can choose not to be defined by this rupture, but rather to incorporate it as part of an ongoing relationship. We hope that the hurt we have experienced will not become the pattern, even as we sense its potential contribution to the depth and substance of our relationship.

Genuine forgiveness is not easy. In order to forgive, we must experience our pain and face the offense that caused it. We must be willing to test our hurt to determine whether our feelings of anger are justified. If we submit our anger to this kind of scrutiny, we may find that we are in the wrong. Perhaps we have misjudged another's motives or overreacted to an event. Then we must decide whether we want to acknowledge our mistake or to nurse our anger and shun forgiveness.

Even when our cause is just, the reflection that forgiveness requires may reveal ways in which we have contributed to the hurt. In adult life, most interactions are conjoint, with each of us contributing to the problems that develop. In few situations is one party solely to blame. Unfortunately, seeing ourselves as innocent victims may be more important to us than risking the self-examination that forgiveness asks of us.

Genuine forgiveness also robs us of our hurt. We must surrender this cherished, if painful, souvenir. By letting go, we lose the vengeful sense of moral superiority we have been savoring, even as we regain the energy squandered in our resentment. In a sense, forgiveness evens the score, for it undercuts the sense that we have something to hold over the other person. In forgiving, we begin anew, perhaps humbled but also hopeful.

Forgiveness is hard to give and hard to receive. To accept forgiveness, we must revisit the pain we have caused. We have to acknowledge our responsibility and admit where we were in the wrong. It is humbling to need forgiveness, and to deny everything may seem easier than reaching out in love. To accept forgiveness is to acknowledge our guilt, not only to ourselves, but to the other person as well.

Sometimes, after an initial rush of anger, we recognize that our accusation is misdirected or that our sense of injury is exaggerated. As we come to this new understanding, we often feel our anger dissolve on its own, but forgiveness asks more of us than this. Forgiveness moves us beyond anger, but only after we have moved through it, and this involves both judgment and choice. Truly to forgive, we must revisit the anger and test our sense of injury and blame. But when our anger registers genuine hurt, forgiveness does not allow our focus to remain there. In forgiveness, we choose not to retaliate with the punishment to which we feel entitled, but to respond with compassion and concern. Such compassion is seldom a companion to our early anger, and, like genuine forgiveness, this impulse arrives more often as grace than as a direct result of our choice.

Forgiveness is not always dependent on an apology from the person who has harmed us. We can learn to forgive a parent now dead, a former spouse who has deserted us, and even those who choose to remain our enemies. Therapists remind us that forgiveness marks a crucial step in an injured person's recovery, even if the wrongdoer expresses no regret.

Forgiveness does not always lead to reconciliation, to a healed relationship or to a restored friendship. The work of forgiveness can begin in a single heart, but rebuilding a relationship requires mutual commitment. Such reconciliation is not always possible, and sometimes is not even desirable. The process of forgiveness demands that we acknowledge the injury, confront our own involvement in the pain, and commit ourselves to change. It does not demand that we remain in an abusive relationship or return to a situation in which our well-being is at risk. Even as we move toward forgiveness, part of anger's gift may be to energize our resistance and protect us from falling back into patterns that do not lead to more abundant life.

When reconciliation is the goal, forgiveness is a powerful ally. Sometimes forgiveness is the only path to peace. At other times, we cannot talk enough, explain enough, or express enough regret to bring about reconciliation. The harm has been too great, and the distance between us is now too vast for us to bridge. In these situations, we recall that forgiveness is more than a personal achievement; it is a gift and a grace that we must await in hope.

JESUS' CALL TO FORGIVENESS

If another disciple sins, you must rebuke the offender, and if there is repentance, you must forgive. And if the same person sins against you seven times a day and turns back to you seven times and says, "I repent," you must forgive. (Lk 17:3–4)

Jesus repeatedly emphasized forgiveness, and the promise of God's forgiveness is among the most startling of Christian hopes. We discover that we have the power to change the past! After a severe injury, our hearts tend to harden. Recovering from a failed relationship, we stoically shrug and say, "It happened; there's nothing more that can be done about it." The gospels reveal that we can forgive even ancient wounds; these accounts of Jesus' life prompt us to expect the extraordinary even from ourselves. In the

strength of love, we contradict the power of the past and neutralize the force of its failures.

In Jesus' life, forgiveness took on an importance that even his
followers found difficult to accept. Jesus overturned the religious
wisdom of his day by insisting that virtue was found less in upright
observance of the law than in forgiving one another. A woman
caught in adultery was brought into a public square to be shamed
and even stoned, but Jesus seemed uninterested in her punishment. His care for the woman suggested three elements of repentance: acknowledging the wrong, letting it go, and turning our
lives away from future wrongdoing. Jesus did not invent forgiveness, but he underscored its power, announced that it was available
to all, and made this virtue an identifying characteristic of those
who would follow him. We, too, must be willing to forgive our enemies, our friends, and even ourselves.

Forgiveness is a movement of *eros*. Its energy alters the nature
of Christian community, inviting us to see ourselves as a gathering
of the wounded and sinful, not just the virtuous. A community
with the power to forgive carries an extraordinary resource. Alive
with this power, Christian community itself becomes a sacrament
of reconciliation.

FOR FURTHER REFLECTION

Take a few moments to become aware of your life these days—
with family and friends, at work, in your church, and in your civic
community.

Recall a recent time when you experienced anger in response to injustice: unfair treatment, dishonest conduct, betrayal of public
trust, contempt for significant values. Let this experience become
full again in your memory.

Then consider these questions:

> In this particular experience, how was your anger an ally?
> What positive results can you trace to your arousal? What
> actions did your anger lead to? What insight did your
> anger provide?

> In this particular experience, how was your anger a
> problem? What negative consequences can you trace to
> your arousal? Was your anger a distraction? Did your
> anger make matters worse?

> What convictions and cautions about the role of anger
> in pursuit of justice can you draw from your own
> experience?

12

Eros of Compassion

PASSION'S BRIDGE TO JUSTICE

But while he was still far off, his father saw him
and was filled with compassion;
he ran and put his arms around him and kissed him.
— Luke 15:20

Jesus told the story of a wayward son who returned to the father he had sorely wronged. The son's homecoming took a surprising turn when his father did not respond in anger or withhold his welcome until after he had received an apology. He seemed uninterested in pointing out the error of his son's ways or in ensuring that he had learned his lesson. Instead, the father rushed out to meet his son, overjoyed at his return. Sensing the boy's humiliation and despair, his father treated him as an honored guest and planned a great celebration.

Jesus tells us that this is what God is like. God receives us not as judge but as *Abba*, an extravagantly loving parent who wants our care for one another to show the same abundant concern. What God asks of us is not sacrifice, but mercy. The lives of the godly will be marked not so much by the conspicuous good deeds of the righteous as by the humble compassion of those who respond to the world's needs.

Compassion is an experience of *eros*. Ordinarily, we think of compassion as commiseration, as feeling the suffering of another person, but compassion has a more expansive meaning. With this emotion, we may enter into the full realm of passion—delight and confusion, anger and joy. By the bridge of imagination, we cross over into another's world of feeling. We experience the excitement of our friend's success; we taste the sorrow that fills his heart.

The *eros* of compassion encompasses the many ways in which our hearts go out to others. Nature can also call forth our response. Walking along the seashore, we are drawn slowly into the mood of the breaking waves. An awareness of our union with nature and its unhurried rhythms is part of compassion. We embrace a part of the world that does not simply revolve around us.

Standing by a polluted stream, we feel another emotion, one closer to the ordinary meaning of compassion. Contemplating this damaged resource, we experience regret and sorrow, tinged with a sense of responsibility. Polluting this river dirties our own lives; even if we do not live near the stream, we share its life and its ruin. This mood of regret stirs us to reverse the destruction.

Compassion has special poignancy when we move toward those in distress. The Latin word *misericordia* captures this face of *eros* —we act mercifully when we have a heart (*cor*) for those in misery. Compassionate acts link us in solidarity with those who suffer and challenge the barriers that isolate us from one another. As we cross these boundaries, compassion opens us to a previously hidden kinship.

It is easy to turn away from a stranger who suffers. Many of us have learned to regard most other people as strangers or outsiders. The *eros* of compassion gives us a new way of seeing that allows us to recognize a person in need as "our kind." We share a common humanity, a shared vulnerability, and we are equally loved by God. Responding to this kinship, compassion teaches us to act with kindness.

Often we first have to act "as if" those who are different—a member of the parish who is developmentally disabled, a refugee family recently arrived in the neighborhood, an undocumented laborer seeking work—are, in truth, our kind. When we repeatedly act in this way, a transformation occurs. "Those people" gradually become "our people," and their passions now seem very similar to our own.

The connections between compassion and kinship become clear in the parable of the Good Samaritan (Lk 10:30–37). A man of Israel lay wounded by the roadside, a victim of highway robbery. Two of his own kind—first a priest and then a member of the privileged class—come upon the stricken man and pass him by. He is an inconvenience—a tragic case, perhaps, but none of their affair. A third traveler approaches. He belongs to a tribe despised by the Jews; he is a Samaritan, an outsider, their enemy, but this foreigner responds with compassion. Moved by the wounded man's plight, the stranger interrupts his journey. He dresses the man's wounds, takes him to an inn, and pays for his care. Ethnic hatred, national rivalry, and a heritage of mutual suspicion are set aside to address this person's need.

Jesus offered this parable in answer to questions about kinship: "Who is my neighbor?" Who has a right to my resources and a claim on my care? Jesus responded by showing us how a neighbor acts and inviting us to do likewise.

The story Jesus tells is filled with paradox. Where we expect to see group solidarity in action, we find only indifference. And where hostility would not surprise us, we find genuine concern. In the actions of this outsider, we see what constitutes kinship. Only he "was moved with compassion when he saw him." Our neighbor, then, is the person in need. Our kind are not only those linked to us by ties of blood or belief, but all those whose pain and hope we dare to share. Compassion creates kinship. In response to the question, "Who is my neighbor?" the parable shifts the focus. We are called to *become* a neighbor by letting ourselves be moved to action by another's plight. Compassion carries us beyond the surge of sympathy toward healing acts.

HOW COMPASSION DEVELOPS

Humans display an innate responsiveness to other people's pain. We see this even in small children. In a nursery school, one child will console another who seems sad. On a neighborhood playground, a toddler who falls down begins to weep, and another child in the vicinity will begin to cry in sympathy. Children spontaneously respond to animals in pain. The human psyche seems to come equipped to notice and respond to the pain around us.

In growing up, most of us developed strategies that sheltered us from that pain. If we lived in a dysfunctional family, such strategies may have helped us survive. Even in less toxic settings, we find ways to distance ourselves from other people's distress. For many people in the helping professions—medical personnel and pastors, counselors and other caregivers—learning to moderate their feelings can be helpful in situations where they must carry out other, more demanding, responsibilities. But denying our sensitivity can erode the quality of our care. Compassion invites us to let down our defenses and embrace the empathic responses that reverberate in our hearts.

If we pursue the practice of compassion we are going to be disturbed, not only in our daily schedules but also in our spirit. Sometimes the only way to recognize another's need is to enter into that person's pain. Then we are challenged to put aside our protective barriers, let down our guard, and allow ourselves to feel. Here we pray with the prophet Ezekiel, begging God to replace our hearts of stone with hearts of flesh.

Our prayers acknowledge that compassion comes as gift, an erotic grace with transforming effects. The *eros* of compassion moves us to recognize the one who suffers as no longer a stranger but as neighbor, as kin. Compassion empowers us to act with special sensitivity in responding to concrete needs in ways that preserve the dignity of those in distress. Compassion opens us to the pain of the world even as it undermines our false sense of separateness and security.

How Compassion Can Fail

Compassion is a powerful emotion, a social instinct meant to link us to others in empathy and action. Compassion fails when our arousal is disconnected from effective response. Our emotions are stirred, but they lead nowhere. Our tears do not overflow into action; our feelings do not impel us to change anything. We remain stranded in the privacy of our hearts. Then the rich virtue of compassion degenerates into sentimentality.

A second way in which compassion fails is through pity, which often has about it the taint of condescension. We feel concern for others, but we do so from a position of moral superiority; we "descend" to feel sorry for the less fortunate. Reaching down with pity toward these lowly folk, we reinforce the differences between us. In Fritz Perl's words, we pity those who are not "our own serious rivals."

Pity does not heal the gap between people; pity accentuates it. Our seeming generosity reinforces our advantaged position and highlights our superiority. In pity, we show concern within a context that involves no risk and expects a payback in gratitude. An essential element of compassion—its vulnerability—is curiously absent. We help others without identifying with them. Such pity is, at best, compassion compromised.

COMPASSION AS AN ALLY OF JUSTICE

The biblical call to justice has deeply erotic roots. "Blessed are those who hunger and thirst for justice, for they will have their fill" (Mt 5:6; authors' translation). In his Sermon on the Mount, Jesus does not define or explain justice. Instead, he uses the more erotic images of hunger and thirst. For those who follow Jesus, justice is as basic as daily bread and its lack registers in us as physical distress.

Justice is a core virtue in both Christian tradition and American life. For Christians, justice has a privileged place in moral life; for Americans, justice is a central ideal of democracy. Yet justice, despite its wide appeal, remains elusive. How shall we find our way to justice for all?

For centuries, Western philosophers have used the tool of reason to fashion arguments and provide demonstrations of what justice demands. Reason illumines, but it does not persuade; it clarifies the circumstances that surround justice, but does not always move us toward just action. Christian leaders have sometimes drawn on the powerful emotion of guilt: Act with honesty and rectitude . . . or experience guilt over your deficient behavior. Yet neither reason alone nor recognition of guilt seems to have led us very far along the path to a more just world.

Could it be that the path to justice lies along a more erotic trajectory—in the ability to imagine others as like ourselves? Karen Armstrong suggests that justice is the public face of compassion. Perhaps it is *eros* that links these two potent virtues.

A common cultural vision of justice often masks this link. In Western social theory, justice depends on three core principles: fairness, universality, and individual rights. First, justice demands that people be treated fairly. Democracy, for example, intends that the benefits and burdens of society should be shared by all citizens. Laws are enacted to ensure this equal treatment, and justice requires that these laws be applied without bias. Second, this Western understanding of justice rests on respect for universally valid principles. Laws are derived from general norms, and are understood to apply in all cases. In this sense, justice is blind to particular circumstances.

The expectation of fair treatment is linked to the Western vision of individual rights. Basic rights—such as the right to life, liberty, privacy, freedom of assembly, and freedom of religion—are understood as part of what it means to be human. These essential rights are "inalienable" in that they cannot legitimately be taken away by governmental power. In fact, the legal system's purpose is to protect and promote these basic individual rights.

This understanding of justice is one of Western culture's great achievements. The safeguards it provides to personal freedom and social equality are indispensable. Still, there are always limits to how well this vision is realized in actual practice. Critics point out that contemporary Western ideals of justice emphasize sameness and separation. Sameness means that the law's general principles should be applied equally to everyone. Separation means that the legal system is set up to defend individual rights and protect personal autonomy.

Not all cultures understand justice in this way. In many societies —across history as well as today—justice is more explicitly linked with social well-being. Laws are written more to promote communal harmony than to protect private rights. Even in the West, Aristotle's classic discussion of civic virtue stressed commitment to the common good. In drawing on the theological heritage of Thomas Aquinas, Pope John Paul II linked justice to the virtue of solidarity as "a firm and persevering determination to commit oneself to the common good; that is to say, to the good of all and of each individual." Recognizing these alternate voices does not deny the value of the modern Western vision of justice, but it helps us to appreciate its limits as well as its strengths.

The Bible testifies to an expanded vision of justice. The biblical understanding of justice, ethicist John de Gruchy insists, is "inseparable even if distinguishable from love." Justice finds fulfillment in mercy, a heartfelt response that moves beyond cautious calculation. Mercy responds in personal and particular ways, sensitive to the unique situations of those in need. The biblical vision emphasizes our essential interrelatedness.

Jesus embraced the special vision of the world that was Israel's heritage. This legacy teaches us that the orphan and the widow are not outcasts, but family; that immigrants and refugees are, finally, part of our community. Jesus called this fragile but persistent vision— in which justice is joined by compassion—the reign of God.

THE BIBLE TUTORS THE IMAGINATION

The Bible does not provide us with an explicit code to follow, or a script that tells us what to do in every complex circumstance of our lives. Instead, as William Spohn reminds us, the stories and symbols in sacred scripture "encourage certain scenarios." The stories of Jesus repeatedly seeking out the sinner and the outcast, his compassion for those afflicted in body or spirit, his constant call for forgiveness, "become scenarios for action by evoking affective energies in distinctive ways." These affective energies insert us again into the world of *eros*. As we return to these gospel stories, we bathe our imaginations in a biblical vision of reality. Through these dramatic parables and compelling images, the sacred scriptures slowly give a distinctive shape to our response. The work of the biblical stories is not to burden us with exact rules, but to bend our hearts toward more just and compassionate ways of living.

Tutoring our imaginations begins with the Bible's vision of the "other." Our Jewish ancestors retained searing memories of slavery in Egypt and exile in Babylon. Yahweh urged them to keep these memories fresh. Amid the many commandments in the book of Exodus, this demand was evidently worth repeating: "You shall not oppress a resident alien; you know the heart of an alien for you were aliens in the land of Egypt" (Ex 23:9).

And yet...despite these injunctions to respect and care for others who were suffering the displacement they had themselves once endured, the Israelites were also struggling to preserve their religious identity among a host of tribes with different gods and practices. Threats from and hostilities with these tribes sometimes led to violent feelings toward religious "others." This hostility endures today in violence among ethnic groups in many places around the world.

What are we to make of the "other"? How are we to act toward those whom we judge to be different from us? In the first decade of the twenty-first century, intense questions about the "other" have taken center stage. What shall America do about the immigrants who seek to share the benefits of our national life? We are descendants of immigrants, but we are newly cautious about allowing others to participate in our commonwealth. The terror of 9/11 and subsequent conflicts throughout the world have raised the profile of the foreigner and the alien, who are portrayed in fevered imaginings as dangerous threats to our safety. What are we to do about those who are different from us?

Philosopher Emmanuel Levinas has been a great apostle of the "other." In the aftermath of the Second World War, Western nations were flooded with displaced persons, many of whom were survivors of the Holocaust. As a Jew in post-war Europe, Levinas was intensely aware of ways in which he was different. He insisted that, if philosophy were to be relevant in such a world, it would have to find its starting point in ethics, and ethics would have to begin with recognition of the "other."

Levinas's starting point is stark and direct. The first words of the other are, "I am not you; do not kill me." The "other," Levinas argues, intrudes into our lives, making us uncomfortable and raising questions we would rather ignore. The presence of the "other" disturbs the order, reason, and control we so cherish. If we do not begin our ethical reflection with attention to those who make our lives uncomfortable, neither our morality nor our philosophy will be genuine.

GOD APPROACHES US AS "OTHER"

Near the end of Matthew's gospel, we come to a remarkable parable that reveals the spiritual depth of compassion. In the final reckoning, Jesus says, God judges us according to our care for those who are most vulnerable. In this parable, the Lord says to the just: "I was hungry and you gave me food, I was thirsty and you gave me something to drink, I was a stranger and you welcomed me, I was naked and you gave me clothing, I was sick and you took care of me, I was in prison and you visited me" (Mt 25:35–36).

Those who hear the Lord's words in the parable are confused. "When did we see you hungry or thirsty or naked?" The Lord responds, "Just as you did it to one of the least of these who are members of my family, you did it to me" (Mt 25:40).

Perhaps this gospel writer was intentionally recalling God's earlier insistence on justice. Dismayed by their empty displays of piety, the Lord had chastised the Israelites "Such fasting as you do today will not make your voice heard on high. . . . Is this not the fast that I choose: to loose the bonds of injustice? . . . Is it not to share your bread with the hungry, and bring the homeless poor into your house; when you see the naked to clothe them?" (Isa 58:4, 6–7). From these biblical roots has grown the Judeo-Christian concern to care for "the least"—the marginal and most vulnerable members of society.

Reason and law are powerful guardians of a just society, and the painful emotion of guilt alerts us when we act unjustly. But it is the erotic power of the imagination that motivates us to build a more compassionate world. The Bible tutors our imagination, instilling images of a way of life that rises above chronic enmity and revenge. In this vision, strangers and aliens are recognized as our sisters and brothers. No longer feared as potential contaminators of our precious integrity, they may now be embraced as worthy companions. The *eros* of compassion opens pathways to this more generous life.

FOR FURTHER REFLECTION

Recall a time when you witnessed an act of genuine compassion. This action may have been offered directly to you in a time of need. Or a memory may come of your compassionate response to someone else. Perhaps you were simply an observer on the scene when genuine compassion was displayed. Take a few moments now to bring this experience vividly to mind—the persons involved, the circumstances, the setting, the actions, the emotions, the outcome.

Then consider:

> How does this experience connect with or confirm your understanding of compassion?

> How does this experience expand your understanding of compassion?

> Does this experience carry new insight for you into links between compassion and justice?

PART FOUR

THE RHYTHMS OF EROS

*Eros is a vital energy that surges and subsides
throughout our lives.*

*On the spiritual journey, we learn to
attune ourselves to these changing rhythms.*

*Presence and absence is a common rhythm,
as we shift from attentive awareness
to seasons of separation and loss.*

*Holding on and letting go is a familiar movement,
as lively engagements give way to
necessary departures.*

*Feasting and fasting is yet another rhythm,
as we move from delight and pleasure into
periods of solitude or sorrow.*

*In the midst of these movements we encounter
the shadows of eros,
the ways in which this volatile energy can go awry.*

*The energy designed by God to move us toward abundance
can be diverted along paths that do not lead to life.*

13

Presence and Absence

HONORING LIGHT AND DARKNESS

A little while and you will no longer see me;
and again a little while and you will see me.
— John 16:19

T he cultivation of *eros* begins in recognizing its rhythm in our
lives. *Eros* does not flow in a steady stream, but surges and
subsides in alternating currents. Sexual passion peaks and recedes;
the *eros* of curiosity stirs and settles. Every life knows the cyclic
movement from rest to high excitement, followed by a return to
quiet calm. A growing ability to tune our lives to these elusive
rhythms supports both psychological health and spiritual maturity.

Sacred scripture charts these rhythms. In community crises of
challenge or hope, in personal mood swings from elation to depression, the biblical narratives invite us to celebrate the movement that shapes the life of faith. At the heart of this dynamic lies
the core tension between life and death. The Bible frames this
root rhythm from the creation story that opens the book of Genesis to the searing death of Jesus recorded near the end of the
gospels. This rhythm preoccupies each of us, as we look back over
our lives and look forward to the certainty of our deaths. Biblical
parables remind us that this paradox stands at the center of our
story of faith: "Unless a grain of wheat falls into the ground and
dies, its remains just a single grain. But if it dies, it bears much
fruit" (Jn 12:24).

143

The gospel record of Jesus' life and death announces a more bewildering truth. In human experience, there are values worth living for; even more startling, there are values worthy dying for. How can this be? What could be more important than life, we may ask. Yet it is likely that each of us can name values—our children, our country, our integrity—that we would willingly place ahead of our own survival. The gospel also reminds us that we can so love our lives that we lose them (Jn 12:25). We can cling to our own desperate survival and end up losing what we most cherish.

These realizations are not unique to Christians. The Chinese philosopher Xunzi wrote, "He who seeks only to preserve his life at all costs will surely suffer death." Mencius, a near-contemporary of Xunzi, said:

> I love life, but there are things I love more than life;
> that is why I do not cling to life at any cost.
> I hate death, but there are things I hate more than death;
> that is why there are some troubles I will not avoid.

In the Song of Songs, we read that "love is as strong as death." In the story of Jesus' life, we see that love may be even stronger than death. Jesus' life came to a terrible end, but his followers experienced his continued presence among them. This experience shapes the Christian awareness of the mysterious rhythms of dying and coming to life.

Eros flows rhythmically through our lives. Presence alternates with absence, holding on with letting go, feasting with fasting. Christians experience these as *saving* rhythms. If we can attune our lives to these alternating currents of *eros*, these shifting movements of grace, we may find that our lives are saved even in the midst of suffering and death.

RHYTHMS OF PRESENCE AND ABSENCE

May the Lord bless you and keep you;
May the Lord make his face to shine upon you

And be gracious to you.
The Lord lift up his countenance upon you
And give you peace. (Num 6:24–26)

When we are surrounded by loved ones, we are content and at peace. But there are days—and seasons—when we are removed from their presence. Work, travel, illness, or depression may absent us from those we most care about. Cultivating the vital energy of *eros*, we become more reliably present to others in love and compassion. We realize that some absences are not of our making and, however painful, must simply be borne. Thus are we educated into the rhythms of presence and absence.

Our religious ancestors experienced the pendulum swing of presence and absence even in their relations with God. They remembered a time when "the Lord used to speak to Moses, face to face, as one speaks to a friend" (Ex 33:11). Yet in this same chapter we read of another time, when God seemed to require absence, "You cannot see my face; for no one will see me and live" (Ex 33:20). Our lives of faith, like theirs, are governed by this paradoxical rhythm of presence and absence.

Jewish and Christian spirituality celebrate the mystery of God's presence in the world. In faith, we are emboldened to approach this mysterious "Other," whose extraordinary power lies at our origins, animates our every breath, and extends beyond our earthly existence.

PRESENCE IN ABSENCE

At the dawn of Hebrew history, Abraham and Sarah experienced Yahweh's presence as they offered hospitality to three strangers. These mysterious guests revealed that, despite the fact that Abraham and Sarah were advanced in years, they would bear a child whose descendants would become a great nation (Gen 18).

Yahweh's presence appeared again in the desert. After Moses led Yahweh's people out of slavery, they soon found themselves wandering in a vast and arid land. Yet in this hostile climate, lacking sustenance and shelter and sense of direction, they became aware of a protective and guiding power. The book of Exodus speaks of the cloud that guided the people through their desert travail: "Whenever the cloud was taken up from the tent, the Israelites would set out on each stage of their journey; but if the cloud was not taken up, then they would not set out until the day that it was taken up" (Ex 40:36–37). The band of nomads came to recognize the movements of this mysterious power, both its frightening absence and its unpredictable appearance. Later tradition would name this mysterious force *Shekinah* or "Presence." It would lead them from the hostile desert to "a land flowing with milk and honey" and nourish them along the way.

The sacred story of God's mysterious presence in human history continued centuries later in the New Testament memory of Pentecost. After Jesus' death his disciples gathered in an upper room, painfully aware of his absence. For a time they had enjoyed his engaging presence, but now it seemed they were to be left with only memories. In this domestic desert, emotionally depleted and lacking any sense of direction, they suddenly experienced an extraordinary surge of energy, symbolized in the rush of wind and tongues of fire (Acts 2). Their grief at Jesus' absence was transformed into enthusiasm and confidence. A presence that they would recognize as the Spirit of God had entered their lives.

In the many biblical stories of God's presence, we meet again and again the curious theme of God's absence. The sterile, debilitating environment of the desert seemed somehow essential to the Israelites' recognition of God's saving presence. At Pentecost, Jesus' absence made room for the Spirit of God to enter the believing community with new force. The revelation of these stories is that presence often requires absence. For humans, there is no such thing as a guaranteed sense of divine presence, just as we are never fully present and attuned to one another. God's gracious presence in history will always be an epiphany, a presence that appears with surprising illumination out of apparent absence.

Two disciples were returning to their village after witnessing the devastating events of Jesus' death (Lk 24:13). Disconsolate as they walked toward Emmaus, they were joined on the road by a stranger who asked the cause of their sorrow. Then he spoke to them, recalling God's promise of life that is born of death. His words relieved their hearts, and they urged him to join them for their evening meal. As the story tells us, "in the breaking of the bread" they recognized the stranger as Jesus. Then, as suddenly as he had appeared to them, Jesus vanished. The flash of this epiphany—this momentary glimpse of Jesus who comes in the guise of a stranger—did not leave them empty or discontent. Instead, their spirits were revived: "Were not our hearts burning within us!" The flame was both *eros* and grace.

The mystery of God's presence and absence does not end with the biblical accounts. Christians continued to break bread together in memory of Jesus' final meal with his companions. The eucharistic liturgy that developed from this early ritual is itself a celebration of presence and absence. The early Christian communities recognized that when they broke bread in Jesus' memory (that is, in his absence), Christ became present to them in ways that enlivened their spirits. After this celebration, people returned to their lives nourished and newly energized. As in the Emmaus story, Christ does not linger with us today in a guaranteed sense of presence. But in the breaking of bread at shared Eucharist, Jesus is again present. If this presence is fleeting, it is also enlivening and nourishing. The challenge is to honor the absences that accompany God's presence in our lives.

EVERYDAY ABSENCE

During periods of significant change, we may find ourselves looking back to "better days." In the upheavals of the present moment, we long for times we remember—perhaps through the distorting lens of rose-colored glass—as happier or more stable. Our religious ancestors, adrift in the "freedom" of the Sinai desert, yearned for the consolations of their earlier lives. While they were captives in the "fleshpots of Egypt," at least they had food and shelter. And even in their captivity, their identity was stable—they knew themselves to be slaves.

A certain measure of nostalgia is healthy. Even if we are eager to move on, we often glance back lovingly at earlier or more innocent seasons in our lives. But unchecked, this sentiment can become a means of absenting ourselves from the present. So, although it is suffused with melancholy, nostalgia is sometimes cultivated and cherished. A returning war veteran daily grieves that he and his comrades do not receive the respect due them. A parishioner, resisting the growing pains of the church, insists that an earlier era "had it right." Nostalgia may grow into what one writer has named a "hypochondria of the heart."

Composure, too, can become an exercise in absence. Usually our stance of self-possession—the way we present ourselves to the world—is a healthy social resource. To survive adult life, we develop strategies that sustain our composure in public. Often we are not aware of this resource until our composure suddenly abandons us. We lose our train of thought in the midst of a conversation; we confuse the names of two friends when trying to make an introduction. We are embarrassed and momentarily befuddled—we lose our composure. Most often, we quickly pull ourselves together and continue, chastened by sudden awareness of our vulnerability but sustaining only a surface wound.

Adam Phillips describes composure as a means of *self-holding* that may escalate into *self-hiding*. Many American men report that they have become not only self-possessed but also inhibited. In social interactions they hold themselves slightly aloof, to avoid being caught "off guard." Here the necessary skill of composure serves as protective armor; they project a self-sufficiency that leaves them detached from others and often from their own emotions. Many men see themselves in this familiar scenario: A close colleague, seeing his friend in obvious distress, asks, "How are you?" Automatically—and falsely—the response comes: "I'm fine." The man's heart may be breaking, but a habit of self-possession masks this vulnerability. Composure offers this protection, but at a very high cost.

Garrison Keillor has made a career out of recalling his religious upbringing. He writes about how this background instilled a rigid composure: "You taught me to be nice, so that I am full of niceness, I have no sense of right and wrong, no outrage, no passion." As an adult, Keillor gently mocks his own dysfunction: "I am constantly adjusting my feelings downward to achieve that fine balance of caution and melancholy." Our laughter at Garrison Keillor's stories is often the laughter of recognition.

When caution regularly displaces curiosity, this signals that composure has put our vitality at risk. Curiosity is an erotic energy, an impulse that leads us beyond ourselves into the experiences and relationships through which our lives will flourish. When caution cancels curiosity, we may survive, but we will not thrive. We will miss—that is, absent ourselves from—much of the wonder of life.

We invent many ways to absent ourselves from our lives, but nature conspires to make us present again. One of the methods nature uses is beauty. Beautiful things attract our attention, arrest our restlessness, and pull us into the here and now. Gazing at a magnificent city skyline or a lovely delicate flower we are rescued, for the moment, from our distractions and worries. While we gaze, we are absorbed; we are here.

Literary critic Elaine Scarey describes the force of beautiful things: "It is as though beautiful things have been placed here and there throughout the world to serve as small wake-up calls to perception, spurring lapsed alertness back to its most acute level." The power of something beautiful to wrench us into the present is not just a matter of aesthetics. An erotic bond links beauty with care. When we become aware of a beautiful vase or a fragile ancient manuscript or—especially—a lovely child, we give greater attention to its safety and survival. "Noticing its beauty increases the possibility that it will be carefully handled."

GENEROUS ABSENCE

The story of Pentecost—Jesus' absence from the early Christian community and the appearance of the Spirit—alerts us to an intriguing dynamic that we might call "generous absence." Jesus absented himself from his community of followers, leaving a void of leadership. In the midst of painful emptiness, the disciples had to decide how to preserve and preach the values they had learned from Jesus. Through this crisis—Jesus' generous absence—these followers themselves became leaders.

The mysterious rhythms of presence and absence are repeated in lives today. A team of campus ministers—a priest and two lay persons—work well in a university setting. The priest is a dynamic and gifted leader, and his younger colleagues delight in assisting him in their shared work with the students. One day, the priest is transferred to another assignment, and the two remaining staff members are devastated. What will they do without their leader's charismatic insights and talented guidance? They grieve their loss and begin making new efforts to respond to the students' continuing needs. To their great surprise, these lay ministers find themselves up to the challenge. While they were depending on the talented priest's pastoral leadership, they had not recognized—had not needed—their own resources. Now, deprived of his gifts, they became aware of their own. In the leader's generous absence, their own strengths for ministry emerge.

PRACTICES OF PRESENCE

The rhythms of presence and absence often seem to carry their own energy. Yet we are not mere victims of this movement; we can choose to engage in practices that can make us more present and give us greater tolerance for unavoidable seasons of absence.

The liturgies of the Christian life are designed for this. Liturgical rituals can teach us ways of being more present to God and more grateful for God's many gifts. In rituals of grieving, we learn to acknowledge the losses and mistakes of our life without being overwhelmed by them.

A spirituality of presence also invites us to become more attentive to ourselves, the unique and particular (thus peculiar) person we are called to be. Being more at home in our bodies, with their own cycles of activity and rest, may be one benefit of this attentive presence. Another gift may be our increasing comfort with solitude.

As our capacity for solitude grows, we learn to befriend absence. We become more comfortable with quiet and come to treasure time apart. Facing the negative emotions or painful memories that arise in the void of absence, we recognize that emptiness also creates a space for significant blessings. The absence that accompanies a loved one's death invites us to accept the loss, as we create a new presence in cherished memories. Absence provides a space for gratitude, for acknowledging the friends and values that have blessed our lives.

Anyone who prays must befriend absence, since God's silence is sometimes louder than our prayers. But as we become familiar with absence, God's silence need not sadden us. We remember God's presence in the past and look forward in hope to the return of that presence. In the meantime, we can tolerate the stillness.

FOR FURTHER REFLECTION

In a mood of quiet reflection, recall a time of God's special presence to you, a time when you were profoundly aware of the reality of God in your life. Take time to let the memories become rich and full again. After spending some moments in this recollection, name a gift or grace that you experienced in this awareness of God's presence. You may wish to bring this reflection to a close with the following prayer.

Prayer of Presence

God of Israel, God of Jesus, your name is Shekinah, Presence.
We feel your saving presence in our bodies, our emotions, our hopes.

You appear in deserts and oases, in crises and in quiet meals.
Your epiphanies calm our fears and heal our shame.

Help us to recognize you in all your faces—
in the flesh as well as in the spirit, in Eros as well as in Logos.

Help us remember that Jesus is God's desire in the flesh,
God's body language.

Make us alive to our world, and through it, alert to your presence.

Continuing the reflective mood, recall your experience of the absence of God; be gentle with this recollection, honoring the movement of your own life's journey. After some moments in recollection, name a gift or grace that was part of this mysterious absence of God. You may wish to bring this recollection to a close with the following prayer.

Prayer of Absence

God of presence, help us to bear your mysterious absence.

Help us through the darkness of the nights when we cannot see you,
the discontent of winters when we cannot feel you,
the sorrow of seasons when we cannot hear you.

Attune us to the absence that is generous—
emptying us of a cherished past
in preparation for your surprising future.
Lead us not into despair, but toward the hope of your coming.

14

Holding On and Letting Go

LEARNING THE RULES OF ENGAGEMENT

Conflict is one of the ways we hold those we love.

The energy of *eros* lures us into relationships. In these risky encounters we learn both how to hold others well and how to
relax our grip. The ever-changing challenge of holding and letting
go introduces another rhythm of *eros*.

Human life begins in the first cycle of this erotic rhythm. Our
parents held one another in a fertile embrace that gave us life; nine
months later we were released from the warm sea of our mother's
womb and set out on a new path. From this initial dynamic of
holding and releasing, all our beginnings and endings flow. Moving through life, we learn to embrace new friends, to hold fast to
our values, to chance a new career. We learn to hold on to significant relationships through times of stress and to let go of commitments that have become toxic. Our engagements and farewells
may be fruitful or threatening, graced or grief-ridden. And even as
we cling to loved ones and cherished values, the rhythmic movements of *eros* rehearse the final letting go of our death.

Roberto Unger describes the tension between "holding on"
and "letting go" as a dynamic of maturity through which

> you lose the world that you hoped vainly to control. The
> world in which you would be invulnerable to hurt, misfor-
> tune, and loss of identity. And you regain it as the world

that the mind and the will can grasp because they have stopped trying to hold it still or hold it away.

Maturity invites us to loosen our grasp on the world and on others. It is a matter not of abandoning our commitments or disengaging from the multiple relationships that give us life, but of appreciating the limits—even the illusions—of our control. Letting go of the effort to hold the world still or hold it away we may find, as Unger suggests, that God's world becomes much more available to our embrace.

The rich metaphor of holding encompasses the multiple embraces and commitments that *eros* engenders. Most of us carry warm memories of being held by our parents—our father carrying us, heavy with drowsiness, into the house after a long car trip; our mother holding us in her arms during a childhood illness. We are consoled by memories of the trusting embraces that have been part of a long friendship, and the teachers and mentors who fostered our growth.

But the metaphor of holding sometimes provokes less friendly memories. We may recall that our parents, in fact, did not often hold us with affection. Some of us were held in harmful or punishing ways, by parents or other caregivers who should have protected us. Others were held back from plans and dreams that their families did not dare to support. And even the best embraces have to change in order to survive. Repeatedly we let go of outdated ways of holding one another, so that we may preserve important relationships. Thus a parent becomes an adult friend, a former mentor becomes a colleague.

Rooted in the sensual embraces of sexuality, birth, and family, the metaphor of holding aptly describes the exercise of religious faith as well. Christians recognize that the world is which they live is held and sustained by the loving Creator. The Bible proclaims that "the spirit of the Lord fills the whole world. It holds all things together" (Wis 1:7; authors' translation). Paul, no doubt aware of that passage, applied the metaphor to Jesus Christ: "In him all things hold together" (Col 1:17). And the traditional hymn says it well: "He's got the whole world in his hands."

The image of God's embrace is more than a cosmic metaphor. Christians have traditionally envisioned God as parent and protector. We are sustained in existence not only by a benevolent universe but by a personal and loving God. Confidence in this first and most enduring embrace resonates in the prayer of the psalmist, "My soul clings to you. Your right hand holds me fast" (Ps 63:8).

The metaphor of holding imbues the faith that emerges in our daily efforts to live as Christians. Returning to the gospel stories again and again, we become aware of the hold that Jesus has on our lives. We may be distressed by scandals in the church or disappointed by weak leadership in our parish. But our faith has a wider embrace, encompassing all those bonds of affection and accountability that unite us in Jesus Christ.

Between the sensual embraces celebrated by poets and the spiritual attachments of religious faith lie the everyday embraces through which our lives flourish. Leaving the secure nest of our first family, we venture into a world of new and risky relationships. We fall in love and share the sweet embrace of sexual passion. In our adult work, we establish ties of cooperation and collaboration. Through our relationships of family and friendship we come to know the embrace of commitment, of making promises and holding ourselves and one another accountable. And, before long, inevitably, we are introduced to the painful experience of conflict.

THE EMBRACE OF CONFLICT

In society's expectations, images of harmony abound. Good friends do not quarrel; mature adults do not become angry; lovers live happily ever after. These romantic fantasies, forcefully marketed, promote the ideal of affection without conflict. Still, we have daily experience of our own fumbling efforts to love well, efforts often accompanied by tension and distress. In these threatening circumstances, we learn that conflict is normal in close relationships. In fact, conflict is critical in many areas of life; it is an honorable dynamic of change and growth.

"The art of living is more about wrestling than dancing," the Stoic philosopher Marcus Aurelius insisted. Wrestling and dancing—two very different styles of holding. Each involves an energetic embrace; the energy of *eros* animates both. Our lives will expectably be marked by both types of encounters. Some people actually relish a good struggle; they find the challenge energizing. Disagreements stir them to fight for their most cherished values. For these few, conflict carries a special charge of *eros*.

But many of us cringe at the threat of wrestling in disagreement with another person or in struggle with a persistent problem. Faced with the possibility of conflict with a friend or work colleague, we turn to other responses. One person will be tempted to flee every contest; another will be inclined to quickly seize control of any threatening situation. Those of us tempted to flee the conflict develop subtle means to achieve this goal. We no longer run from the room like frightened children; instead we avoid conflict by using humor or other distractions to divert disagreements. Or we quickly surrender in the face of any potential conflict. "Whatever you want," we habitually say, hoping to avoid a messy confrontation. Unfortunately, such avoidance seldom removes the conflict; it simply postpones it.

Those tempted to seize control develop sophisticated techniques too: tight management and control of the agenda at our meeting leaves possible conflicts off the table. Here the image of dancing comes to the fore: The person who avoids conflict by controlling other people seems to say, "Let's dance." But the real message is: "Let's dance and I will lead." To outside observers, the orchestrated movement in this marriage or work setting may appear to be a well-coordinated dance. But to the spouse or work partner constrained to the other's rhythms, the embrace feels more like wrestling.

A third response to conflict emerges in a mysterious biblical story. In the darkness of night, Jacob wrestles with a fearful adversary (Gen 32:24–32). Unable to escape and unable to vanquish his opponent, he holds on—struggling for life. In the dark Jacob hopes for the dawn that will shed light on his opponent and illumine the meaning of the conflict.

This evocative tale, which speaks to us about Jacob's relationship with God, portrays intimacy through the metaphor of wrestling. For modern readers, the ancient story resonates with the ambiguous embraces of their own lives. Jacob is alone in the dark when something grabs hold of him from behind. Struggling with this unidentified combatant, Jacob demands to know what is wanted of him. He cannot extricate himself from this embrace nor can he control his nocturnal assailant. In the dark these two struggle, with injury and complaint, toward a new day and a changed relationship.

The heart of this story seems to be the ambiguity of this contentious embrace. Jacob is threatened but not destroyed; in the struggle he is seriously injured, but he is also strengthened as he comes to a new sense of himself. In this sweaty embrace, both Jacob and his assailant are changed. Jacob finds his identity challenged; he is renamed Israel ("one who has struggled with God"). He is also seriously wounded and will limp for the rest of his life. But even his powerful adversary (whom he will later recognize as his God, coming now as strange nocturnal threat) is forced to respond. At Jacob's demand, Yahweh surrenders a blessing. This exhausting struggle has altered both combatants; now they embrace in a new way.

As we grow less threatened by conflict, we recognize its central role in Jesus' life and message. His parables—about the poor and the outcast, about hypocritical behavior, about forgiveness—often make us uncomfortable, forcing us to wrestle with their implications for our own behavior. In his final days, especially in his agony on the night before his death, Jesus himself wrestles with life-and-death conflicts. On the cross, his cry, "My God, why have you abandoned me?" acknowledges the depth of the struggle in his heart.

The Christian heritage includes multiple stories of creative conflict that may offer us guidance. In the first generation of faith, Paul and Peter argued fiercely over how to introduce non-Jewish converts into the community (see Gal 2). Would a kosher diet be expected of all who followed the way of Jesus? Was the traditional Jewish practice of circumcision required of new members? The insight born of this conflict gave rise to new possibilities for the Christian tradition, opening the faith to Gentiles and ultimately to the whole world. Here, to be sure, conflict was filled with grace.

ATTACHMENT AND DETACHMENT

Attachment has long suffered a bad reputation in Western culture, where individualism is so highly valued. Americans are encouraged to stand apart and act independently. Christian spirituality has sometimes reinforced this bias, warning that human attachments may distract us from single-minded devotion to God.

The earliest generations of Christians struggled to live their new faith in the midst of the abuses of the Roman Empire. Life in this imperial milieu, involvement in pagan society, and the daily demands of marriage and family all seemed to require too much compromise for a person set on following Jesus. Had not Jesus challenged the rich young man to "leave all" in the pursuit of God? Had he not said to his disciples, "I have called you out of the world?"

As fervent Christians fled from urban centers to desert monasteries, forsaking both marriage and involvement in civic life, a spirituality of detachment emerged. The goal of the early ascetical movement was admirable, alerting Christians to ways in which everyday attachments may devolve into toxic entanglements. The hope was to free oneself from any involvement that would bind the heart and distract from God.

However, detachment fails as a spiritual discipline when we become too good at it. At the Second Vatican Council the Catholic Church publicly recognized that it had distanced itself from contemporary society, becoming too detached from the developments and demands of the modern world. Catholics were now encouraged to embrace this world, in both its sorrows and its joys. Less concerned that such embraces might compromise the commitment to holiness, the faith community retrieved its ancient convictions: God's attachment to the world, celebrated in Jesus as the Word-made-flesh; humanity's attachment to creation, recognized in our shared responsibility for it.

Cultural ideals of autonomy linked to religious ideals of detachment may leave us wary of making commitments. Our commitments in marriage and family life, our dedication to vocation and career are, of course, attachments. Without the willingness to risk ourselves in these long-term engagements, our lives will not be fruitful. Honoring these attachments, even in the midst of difficulties, evokes the robust resource of fidelity; in the face of the challenges of change we can hold fast to valued commitments. So, we recognize that faith and hope are themselves attachments. Religious faith attaches us to God and to the values Jesus proclaimed; in religious hope we cling to the gospel's vision of a world transformed, even when evidence in its support seems scarce.

The final challenge to our vital attachments is knowing when to let go. We face this especially in the projects we have initiated or pioneered. After a period, we sense that it may be time to let others assume the responsibility for these projects. Perhaps younger colleagues are already hinting that they are ready to take charge. The one reliable principle is that this suggestion will always seem premature. Remember the joke in which the parent cautions the offspring: "It is too early for you to leave home. You are still young. There is a dangerous world out there. You are only thirty-five years old." The invitation to let go always comes too early!

Here, as elsewhere, the gospels guide us. Jesus, in his premature death, absented himself from the community of his followers. Bereft of Jesus' presence and guidance, these first Christians felt abandoned. Then, through the Spirit's power at Pentecost, the disciples discovered their own gifts and authority. In Jesus' generous absence, they became reliable leaders in the community of faith.

This same scene takes place every day in families and church and society, as aging parents, senior teachers, generous leaders let go of projects that are far from finished. Now the next generation is given a chance to assume responsibility. The movement of holding on and letting go continues in the alternating currents of attachment and detachment. Thus the rhythms of *eros* govern our progress through the mysteries of adult life.

FOR FURTHER REFLECTION

Bring to mind an experience of "holding on" that has been life-giving for you.

What vital *attachment*—to a person, a value, a commitment—was involved here?

What blessings came through this effort to stay connected?

Bring to mind an experience of "letting go" that has been life-giving for you.

What *disengagement* or *separation* was demanded of you?

What graces have been part of your experience of detachment?

15

Feasting and Fasting

NOURISHING THE SPIRIT

On this mountain the Lord of hosts will make for all peoples
a feast of rich food,
a feast of well-aged wines.
— Isaiah 25:6

The disciplines of feasting and fasting are celebrated in every culture, as banquets and harvest festivals alternate with seasons of drought and hardship. The Jewish and Christian traditions have placed great importance on this rhythm of *eros* in human life.

The prophet Isaiah is the patron saint of the feast, as he calls forth the image of the final banquet that God has planned for us. Theologian Bernard Lee reflects on the implications of this vision: "It is God's intention for people to enjoy the earth and its abundance. . . . In tasting how sweet the succulent food and fine strained wines are, one can also taste and experience how sweet is God. . . . Plenitude is a disclosure of divine lavishness."

The New Testament records the many festivals and banquets that Jesus attended. Most of us easily recall the wedding feast at Cana, as well as the meal at which a woman of questionable repute poured expensive fragrant oil over Jesus' head. In parables and stories, Jesus spoke about positions of honor at the banquet table, and of inviting people "from the highways and byways" to participate in the feast.

The celebrations attended by Jesus were so frequent that the people around him took notice. Impressed by the ascetical lifestyle of John the Baptist, they voiced their concern: "John's disciples are always fasting and saying prayers, and the disciples of the Pharisees, too, but your disciples eat and drink" (Lk 5:33). Jesus' reply points to a rhythm built into life: "You cannot make wedding guests fast while the bridegroom is still with them, can you? The day will come when the bridegroom will be taken away from them, and then they will fast in those days" (Lk 5:34–35).

In the early centuries of Christianity, fasting became a regular and sometimes extreme practice of monastic life. Feasting fell out of fashion as a religious discipline, as Christians judged that "the time to fast" had arrived. Gradually the eucharistic banquet commemorating Jesus' final meal with his friends evolved into a highly restrained ritual, and its weekly communal celebration eventually became known as "a day of obligation." The ideal of virginity and the later discipline of celibacy attached to priesthood in the Western church prescribed a strict fast from sexual activity. In Christian life today, we are returning to a deeper appreciation of the rhythms of feasting and fasting. These are complementary dynamics, each an important manifestation of *eros* in our daily lives.

WELCOME TO THE FEAST

Public festivities grace the yearly calendar in every nation. At harvest festivals, we recognize both survival and bounty. Feasts and carnivals testify that the human spirit needs regularly to indulge. In the feast, we do more than simply take in nourishment; we make a celebration of our eating. While the food satisfies our nutritional needs, the festivity nourishes other famished aspects of our lives—especially our hunger for community and delight. Without feasts, our souls begin to starve.

We feast both to celebrate and to give thanks. And at its best, feasting is a disciplined performance; we bring out candles, the special tablecloth, the good wine. A banquet proceeds at a leisurely pace, making "fast food" seem out of place. Since a major portion of our delight comes from sharing the occasion with those we love, we rarely feast alone. A feast is not an orgy; we do not abandon ourselves to food or drink or sex. Genuine feasting, in fact, teaches us to avoid excess. When it degenerates into a display of mindless abandon or conspicuous consumption, a party somehow fails as a feast.

The Christian liturgy offers an example of a holy feast. We use colorful vestments and banners, add incense and song, and celebrate in unison our blessings and our grief. Along with other feasts, liturgical celebrations—when not reduced to repetitive or empty gestures—instruct us in an important truth: feasting is a communal art, not a private indulgence.

We feast not just with food and drink, but with all our senses. Listening to a symphony or attending an opera provides a feast for the soul. At a museum, we feast our eyes on art that others have created. But, plagued by the busyness of our lives, we may fail to feast. Weighed down with work and worry, we insist we have no time for such luxuries. But eventually, deprived of this nourishment, our spirit begins to wither.

Feasting is meant to be a part of our sexual lives as well. Feasting in our sexuality both expresses a basic instinct and celebrates something more. Lovemaking involves us in the shared play of pleasure and we give thanks. Savoring our mutual delight, we recognize that sex serves more than reproduction or private relief. As with food and drink, we learn that the feast is ruined when sex is used manipulatively or its pleasure is abused. In our sexuality, too, the feast refuses both denial and excess.

After they have been married for a while, couples often recognize, somewhat ruefully, a new discipline in their sexual feast. As children and pets populate the household, as everyday errands and second jobs fill the weekly schedules, busy parents check calendars to find time to spend together. Now the spontaneity of earlier romance gives way to the necessity of "scheduled" lovemaking—a new rhythm in the sexual dance of mid-life intimacy.

In the life of *eros*, feasting is not abandonment to the flesh. Feasting as a Christian discipline is a response to the gift of creation. If we carry wounds in our psyche, feasting can be a healing exercise. With courage and support, we slowly relearn the goodness of our sensuality. We devote time to re-creation—through music or exercise or quiet time alone. We prepare a special meal to share with friends. We welcome the reverent touch of massage. As we learn to feast in our erotic lives, pleasure returns to a rightful place of honor.

WELCOMING THE FAST

With its many delights and necessary disciplines, feasting is part of the rhythm of *eros*. This movement of *eros* finds its complement in fasting. Over the centuries, fasting has been seen as an exotic exercise, suited to monks, nuns, and other religious elites, but not to ordinary folks like us. Today, we recognize fasting as an ordinary discipline, part of every life.

In the contemporary retrieval of fasting as a healthy discipline, we find a richer motivation. Fasting is not meant as a repudiation of the body and its passions, nor should it spring from a desire to punish a guilty soul. By fasting we interrupt an ordinary rhythm in our life, so that we may listen to other longings.

Fasting is an exercise of concentration, not deprivation. Our lives are unavoidably filled with a rush of duty and delight; each day overflows with demands of what has to be done. These demands are often good in themselves, but their insistence crowds out other hopes and dreams. To fast is to rest briefly, in the midst of busy lives, in order to attune our hearts to neglected possibilities. Fasting gives us practice in paying attention, so that we may be more present to our heart's desires.

Fasting is long cherished in the traditions of the East. As Western Christians return to the experience, we recognize how strangely nourishing a period of fast can be. Interrupting the ordinary rhythms of our lives makes us more alert, more awake. This may be rooted in the physiology of fasting: jolted by a lack of food, the body goes on alert. But once we have gotten past the initial alarm, we come to appreciate the emptiness—in spirit as much as in body. Those who fast report that their senses are sharpener and their minds are more focused as the distracting burdens of daily routine seem to melt away.

In fasting, we say "no" to some part of our experience in order to protect the deeper "yes" of our lives. This can happen in quite ordinary ways. In order to be fully attentive at an important evening meeting, we skip our usual glass of wine with dinner. Finding that a weekend spent watching televised sports dulls our senses and distracts us from family activities, we cut back on TV time in favor of richer pleasures.

Fasting is an ordinary part of our sexual lives as well. Our partner is away on a business trip, or struggling with illness. So we fast from our regular pattern of love-making. Those who embrace a life of committed celibacy recognize that their fast from sexual sharing benefits from a life enriched by genuine friendship and the sensual delights of music, art, and beauty. Fasting from sexual contact because of a belief that *eros* is evil is not a Christian discipline, but an unhealthy flight from creation.

All of us benefit by fasting from overwork and false guilt. We fast from fears and anxieties that hold us back from taking risks. Fasting from jealousy and envy makes us more generous friends. Our fast is less about avoiding evil or denying ourselves than it is about appreciating easily forgotten goods. Fasting briefly from food reminds us of the many people who go hungry, and this awareness may motivate us to contribute something essential to fellow humans in need. In the early church, "fast days" were communal exercises; by fasting together, an entire religious community reminded itself of less fortunate persons whose fasts were not freely chosen, whose fasts were continuous. Thus fasting was linked to compassion and justice. The disciplines of the fast, like those of the feast, are meant to be communal exercises, not private practices.

Other fasts await us: a friendship is broken or a loved one dies and we are deprived of the grace of these relationships. As we mourn their loss, our fast wears the mask of grief, but even in grief we can detect the rhythms of fasting and feasting. Several years ago, a close friend died from cancer at age forty-five. Her many friends were grief-stricken. Together we entered a prolonged fast, now bereft of her graceful presence. The feast that characterized a lovely friendship had ended.

Several weeks later, friends gathered again at her gravesite for the installation of the headstone. After a brief prayer, many returned to her previous home, where quiet conversation continued the mood of mourning. The following year, on the first anniversary of her death, we gathered again to recall this beloved friend whose life we had all shared. We still remembered her pain and final suffering, but at this time we were finally ready to celebrate with wine and some of her favorite foods. Now we would feast, giving thanks for the privilege of having known and loved this remarkable woman. The fast was coming to an end; the feast began again.

The spiritual discipline of fasting—whether in our diet, or our work rhythms, or our intimate lives—is often a chosen practice. But false fasts can intrude into our lives. Through shyness or shame we can fall into a pattern of avoiding close relationships, holding aloof from contacts that might bring us to life. Or we can descend into the unwanted fast of depression, with vitality and pleasure left behind. The cult of thinness manipulates many young women into exaggerated fasting, leading to eating disorders or other abuse of their bodies. Addictive behavior provides a cruel parody of feasting and fasting. The addict indulges in food or drugs or sex, using pleasure as a distraction from a painful part of life. Then, as shame and remorse accumulate, the addict vows to quit: never another alcoholic drink, binge meal, or visit to a pornographic website. A kind of fast ensues, but does not endure. Soon the vicious cycle of addiction returns, mimicking the vital rhythm of *eros*.

Honoring the rhythms of feasting and fasting bears fruit in graceful habits. These habits—identified in Christian tradition as virtues—develop into reliable strengths, as we befriend the movements of our heart. Finding the rhythms of feasting and fasting that are appropriate for us, we craft the virtue of chastity. For most Christians, chastity is not about sexual abstinence. Instead, chastity finds expression in the blending of pleasure and patience, of intimacy and solitude that fits our own vocation. Chastity entails a reverence for our own bodies that helps us to avoid abuse—whether through unhealthy excess or unholy fasts. With chastity, we show the same respect for the bodies of others. In this reverence, pleasure and responsibility meet in the embrace of *eros* and grace.

FOR FURTHER REFLECTION

Some memorable feasts are long anticipated and well-planned; others arise more spontaneously, sometimes even catching us by surprise. Bring back memories of recent feasts in your own life—times of celebration and delight, of festivity and joy.

> Spend several moments savoring the blessing of these feasts, then let the memories move you toward a prayer of gratitude.

Recall now your experience of fasting, both the fasts that you have chosen and those fasts—or seasons of deprivation—forced on you by circumstances. Revisit one significant memory of a fast, staying alert to its meaning for you now.

> What was the most challenging element in this experience of fasting?

> What contribution has the experience of fasting made to your life?

Now consider the rhythm of feasting and fasting in your experience these days.

> Is the current rhythm satisfying for you?

> If not, what can you do to reach a better balance of feasting and fasting in your life now?

16

Shadows of Eros

VITAL ENERGY GONE ASTRAY

*Eros needs to be disciplined and purified if it is to provide
not just fleeting pleasure, but a certain foretaste of…
that beatitude for which our whole being yearns.*
— Benedict XVI

Eros is volatile, even unruly. It awakens us to romance and love, stirring us with desire for the "beatitude for which our whole being yearns." However, it can also erupt in promiscuity, self-indulgence, and violence. With regrettable ease this vital energy slips from longing for abundant life toward lust for possessions. The deep ambiguity of *eros*—its potential for both creativity and destruction—means that it is an energy that requires careful cultivation. The goal of this care is not to render ourselves less passionate, but to shape our passions in more generous ways. Uncultivated, *eros* may easily spiral down darkened pathways that defeat our own deepest desires.

In every culture *eros* flames out in dramatic fashion in the lives of artists—painters, poets, musicians. These celebrated rebels seem to embrace *eros* to the utmost, beyond the realm of our more ordinary lives. Part of their appeal, especially to the young, comes from the excess: they test the limits by "living large," squandering energy and taking reckless risks. For a short season, these talented lives burn bright and then, too frequently, burn out. This extreme, this shadow side of *eros*, stands as both compelling and cautionary tale for the rest of us.

At the other extreme, some people seem always to approach life with caution. Unsure of their desires or perhaps frightened of their own energy, they remain on the sidelines—reluctant to take risks or to engage new possibilities. At both extremes *eros* goes uncultivated; at both extremes we recognize a shadow side of *eros*.

THE EROS OF CURIOSITY—ITS CULTIVATION AND ITS SHADOWS

Early in life, *eros* surfaces as an enthusiastic raw impulse. Curiosity is one of its liveliest expressions. The infant is fascinated with everything in sight, eager to grasp whatever lies within reach. Puppies display this same energetic interest as they leap through life, poking their noses into everything. With the education of the child and the training of the puppy, we begin to cultivate and direct this vital energy.

The *eros* of curiosity appears in teenagers, now newly interested in their own developing bodies and aroused by the sexual attractiveness of people around them. This curiosity is part of the impulse that moves an adolescent out of self-absorption. Infatuation and romance grow from the *eros* of curiosity, and romance blossoms into an affection that leads to devoted and fruitful love.

The energy of curiosity also fuels a young adult's experimentation in career choices and life values. Curiosity lures us into those tentative choices—"Should I become a scientist? A dancer? A politician? A teacher?"—that will one day result in a worthwhile job or rewarding vocation. With cultivation, the vital energy of curiosity becomes a well-honed resource in adult life.

Curiosity that remains uncoupled to any value may easily drift into "idle curiosity." Here random interest continually samples life, but finds no dwelling place. Disengaged from any lasting focus, our curiosity wavers from interest to interest, finding little satisfaction and bearing no fruit.

In American culture, celebrity-watching is a major form of idle curiosity. Supermarket tabloids and website rumors are dedicated to this pastime; they bear witness to Americans' passion to be "in the know." Voyeurism is a variety of idle curiosity that easily becomes addictive. A person avidly watches the activities of others; peering from a distance, the watcher remains unengaged and safe from the risks of genuine encounter. Gossip feeds on a diet of idle curiosity. Around the water cooler or on the Internet, we trade stories about the downfall of authorities or the indiscretions of colleagues. We exchange snatches of information that pique our curiosity, but the distraction does not nourish us or anyone else. *Eros* has lost its way.

Pornography is a graphic example of curiosity "idling" in sterile distractions. In pornography we turn to an addictive face of *eros* hoping, in Augustine's famous phrase, "to satisfy the insatiable." But the stimulation does not satisfy. Pornography courts arousals that are disconnected from any enduring contact. The arc of healthy *eros* is broken and finds no contentment.

The *eros* of curiosity might develop a very different kind of shadow. A child growing into adulthood may learn to be overly cautious, to hold the world at a safe distance. Gradually, caution displaces curiosity. Garrison Keillor laments the caution engendered by his religious upbringing: "You have taught me the fear of becoming lost, which has killed the pleasure of curiosity and discovery. In strange cities, I memorize streets and always know exactly where I am. Amid scenes of great splendor, I review the route back to the hotel."

A season of depression will also dampen the *eros* of curiosity. Treasured relationships, favorite activities, novel possibilities—all fail to hold our interest when we are deeply depressed. The *eros* of curiosity has simply vanished.

SENTIMENTALITY AS A SHADOW OF COMPASSION

Compassion, too, may fall under the shadow of *eros*. The Chinese sage Mencius judged that compassion was an essential ingredient in human nature. Becoming aware of another's plight, the human heart ignites in spontaneous concern. We move toward those who are bereaved or deprived, looking to offer help and solace. But a shadow looms: This natural inclination for compassion sometimes settles into fruitless sentimentality. Then, from our private safety, we observe life as though it were a soap opera. Crying at all the appropriate scenes, we then wipe away the tears and return to our own concerns. Our emotional response—the *eros* of compassion—does not move us into active engagement. We may weep, but we do not act. Our hearts fill momentarily with sadness, but no practical action follows. Our tears leave the world unchanged. The arousal of compassion opens no pathway to generous care, but dead-ends in our sentimentality. This, too, is a shadow of *eros*.

PLEASURE AND ITS SHADOWS

The experience of pleasure is intense and brief. The delight of a touch or the taste of fine food may be thrilling or profoundly gratifying, but is short-lived. What do we make of the intense fragility of sensual pleasure? How are we to both celebrate and cultivate this experience of *eros*?

Sensual delights often generate longings in us that the pleasure itself cannot satisfy. A loving embrace in a time of loneliness elicits our desire to be held unendingly—a hope that our lover cannot satisfy. Bodily pleasures evoke in us desires and dreams whose range outstrips the humble ability of the senses to fulfill. The intensity and brevity of pleasure do not mean that it is illusory or deceptive. We are simply reminded of how fragile the gift of pleasure is.

Pleasure makes us present to creation. But pleasure may also be recruited to deliver us, for a moment, from difficulties in our lives. In troubled times we are drawn to food, alcohol, and sex, hoping these delights may relieve our distress. And they do, intensely but briefly. So we remain unable to face our distress, and must turn again and again to these pleasures to deliver us. This is the story line of addiction.

In addiction, we recruit pleasure to absent ourselves from our distress. We turn to delights, not in order to help us be more present to our life, but rather to lead us away from our pain. And, inevitably, the pain returns. Now for relief we must turn again to this over-mined source—food, alcohol, drugs, sex—to secure a small measure of amnesia. As we place on sensual delights the burden of our futile search for oblivion, genuine pleasure vanishes from our lives. Poet Donald Hall describes his own struggle with addiction: "Self-medication by alcohol/gave temporary relief/brief lethal holiday/and foretaste of death." Spirituality is about presence; addiction is about absence.

Addiction is not about pleasure. The person who eats compulsively, regularly drinks to excess, promiscuously engages in sex is not smiling. David Mura, writing of his own sexual addiction, notes the conspicuous absence of pleasure: "Often, inside the addict is a boy who did not learn the word pleasure. It lay like a stone on his tongue, hard, without taste, impossible to swallow....When sex entered the boy's life, there was no word for pleasure to name it." Marion Woodman, a therapist who has worked predominantly with women in addiction, sounds the theme of absence: "An addict is not in the body, so the body suffers. Uninhabited. And there's where that terrible sense of starvation comes from."

Pleasure can make us present to our life or temporarily absent us from its demands. The *eros* of pleasure opens pathways to joy and satisfaction; in times of great stress, pleasure may lead us down detours of addiction and destruction. Presence makes us attentive to the range of sensual delights that bless our life, and to the pain that signals injury and danger. This presence to pain is not masochism; paying attention to our distress can lead to strategies for healing and rituals of honoring loss. Instead of absenting ourelves from frightful pain or puzzling pleasure, we are called to become present to the full mystery of our lives.

THE SHADOW OF EROTICISM

Tenderness shapes *eros*, finding fulfillment in mutually satisfying pleasure and devoted love. Paul Ricoeur speaks of tenderness as "sexual energy released from the force of a blind drive; it is sexuality personalized." Eroticism, the restless desire for pleasure without interpersonal communion or mutuality, emerges as a shadow of *eros*. When tenderness is replaced by eroticism, "an egoistic cultivation of pleasure wins out over mutual exchange."

The vital energy of *eros* influences much more than sexuality. *Eros* animates our affections, our work lives, and our civic engagements. *Eros* moves us toward enlivening connections and ignites our desire to make a distinctive contribution in our world. Personal maturity and social well-being depend upon the play of *eros* in all its domains.

Work provides us with purpose and meaning. Creating something beautiful or useful adds significance to our lives; offering a valuable service confirms our participation in society. When our daily work is devoid of meaning—offering us the opportunity for neither connection nor contribution—vitality drains from our lives. Each day we go to our boring jobs, but *eros* does not accompany us.

When people lack a sense of personal worth or social significance in their work, they look elsewhere for connection and delight. Many adults find these vital connections within their expanding family network, as their children become adults and start families of their own. Others commit themselves to volunteer activities or hobbies or travel, connecting again with the *eros* of curiosity. But in our culture many people turn to eroticism, the search for sexual pleasure that can anesthetize the meaningless of work.

A similar shadow of *eros* may fall over civic life, where, as in their work, people desire to feel connected and to make a difference. At a time when politics seems driven by corruption and cronyism, citizen participation becomes pointless. When public life is closed to genuine personal involvement, private compensations multiply.

Eroticism is the restless effort to extract diversion and delight (even if only sexual release) from one area of life when other realms are deeply dissatisfying. Expelled from the workplace and the public sphere, *eros* seeks compensation in the fleeting satisfaction of pornography or prostitution. The exploding presence of pornography on the Internet testifies to this increasing eroticism in private life. But eroticism demands of sex more than it can supply.

INSATIABLE CONSUMERISM

Our cities and our souls are shaped by economic forces
.... Our desires are constantly being stimulated, saturated
by social values. (William Schweiker)

We live in the midst of saturated desires—the "must see" enter-tainment, the "must have" possessions, the "cult of fame" defined by money and prestige. In a flourishing economy, there are always things to buy. The market offers new products and "all new" ver-sions of things we already have. To afford these goods, we must work longer. With increased work hours, we outsource childcare, lawn maintenance, and even food shopping. To pay for these con-veniences, we will need to work even longer hours.

As Americans become better off economically, we have less time for leisure and sleep less well. Our country sustains a negative savings rate; we find it difficult to keep up with bills, mortgages, tuition, and healthcare costs. The marketplace provides no criteria for sufficiency. When is enough *enough*? When can we be satisfied with what we have, willing to rest from the pursuit of more? The-ologian William Schweiker asks: "Can we really forsake trying to understand and transform the forces that are shaping our world and our lives?"

Even Christian values can be hijacked by consumerism. The biblical ideal of seeking life in abundance (Jn 10:10) is trans-formed into an endless quest for more possessions. The holy rest-lessness that has always been a mark of the spiritual quest is transfigured into a restless pursuit of wealth and status. The path-ways down which we pursue these goals do not lead to satisfac-tion. In such a climate, there is little room for reflection on questions of justice, or the plight of those excluded from society's benefits, or sacrifice for the common good. Busy with our own lives and tired from overwork, we have little time to spare for such considerations.

How can we step out of the shadows of a consumer culture? Ancient religious ideals—satisfaction with simple abundance, frugality as an environmental virtue, resistance to the greed that is "a rapacious desire for more than one needs or deserves"—provide thin armor in such culture wars. How are we to distinguish our deepest desires from culturally saturated wants? How shall we, in Tom Beaudoin's words, "integrate who we are with what we buy"?

Wendy Farley offers hope, as she traces links between desire and the traditions of a religious heritage. "Traditions enable us to speak together about this desire and to find ways to live more deeply into this desire." Without these traditions, she continues, "desire is like an arrow shot with enormous power but without much direction." Our hope finds a home in those assemblies—small communities of faith, vital parishes where candid conversation is still possible— where we might "speak together" about both our deepest desires and the "saturated desires" that besiege us on all sides.

The sins of *eros*—the familiar offenses of lust, sexual exploitation, addiction—cast a dark shadow over our world. But theologian Peter Black suggests that we explore not just the sins *of eros*, but sins *against eros*. When we think only of sins *of eros* we are likely to reduce this vital energy to sex. But when we examine sins *against eros*—actions that diminish or defeat the vital energy that the Creator has infused into the world—our vision expands. Black argues that "the major sins against *eros* are the sins against justice, namely, right relationships." Institutional injustice and the hardening of our hearts against compassion: these may be the greatest sins against *eros*.

Every culture and each religious heritage attempts to cultivate the essential energy of *eros*. Uncultivated, our sexual attractions, passionate desires, and eager curiosity may lead us down darkening pathways. The goal is not to lessen our enthusiasm but to find its focus, so that it may be fruitful.

FOR FURTHER REFLECTION

Identify a significant "shadow of *eros*" that is influential in your social experience—in your local neighborhood, or the larger civic
community, or national life. Perhaps one of the dynamics discussed
in this chapter: fascination with celebrity and fame; eroticism and
pornography; consumerism and greed. Or perhaps some other destructive social force.

What do you see as the main sources or supports of this
negative energy, this shadow of *eros* at play in your social
world?

What resources do you recognize in religious institutions
—central beliefs, moral perspective, witness of the
members' lives, organized action—that might respond
to this shadow of *eros*?

Practically, how might the members of your faith
community work to challenge or transform this
shadow of *eros*?

CONCLUSION

The Eros of the Gift

The gifts you have received you should also give as gifts.
— Matthew 10:8 (authors' translation)

O ur story begins with *eros*—the vital energy arousing us to life and drawing us toward fruitful alliances. Our erotic lives include sexuality and much more—the quickening of compassion and curiosity, the stirring of wonder and imagination. In all these guises, *eros* moves us toward generous and fulfilling lives.

Grace names the ways in which we find favor with God and one another, the surprising ways in which we know ourselves to be blessed. In his letter to the Romans, Paul repeatedly describes God's grace as a "free gift." We do not earn the blessings that are the source of every "good and perfect gift." Gracious gifts and graceful gestures transform our lives and fill them with abundance.

On the way to your friend's birthday dinner, you stop at a florist. From the many choices on display, you select half a dozen lilies, pay for them, and leave the shop. Arriving at your friend's apartment, you offer her the flowers. Her eyes light up; she places a hand over her heart and breaks into a broad smile. Her emotional reaction triggers a corresponding set of feelings in you. You are delighted that she is pleased. In this simple gesture, we glimpse the mysterious *eros* of the gift.

Before your purchase, the flowers in the shop were simply commodities waiting to be sold. With your purchase, the flowers

177

take on new meaning; your intention transforms this product into a gift. The Chinese language captures this shift: a mere object (*wu*) is altered by the intentional act of selection (*li*), becoming a gift (*li wu*). In the alchemy of gift-giving, ordinary objects are transformed into something else and something more.

Gifts symbolize the extravagance of creation. While possessions may be purchased, accumulated and saved, gifts escape this calculation of gain and loss. Falling in love, we give extravagant gifts to the beloved. We carefully remove the price tags from our gifts to signal that this exchange is "not about the money." Unlike commodities that are prudently priced to suit the market, the value of gifts points to a world of abundance. Our exchanges of affection and care suggest a source of gifts that may be inexhaustible.

ABUNDANT GIFTS

> Satisfaction derives not merely from being filled, but from being filled with a current that will not cease. With the gift, as in love, our satisfaction sets us at ease because we know that somehow its use at once assures its plenty. (Lewis Hyde)

In his lovely meditation in *The Gift*, Lewis Hyde considers three characteristics. First, gifts are bestowed rather than acquired or achieved. Gifts come to us unearned, as part of a mysterious inheritance. I am surprised to discover a personal talent—for music, or mathematics, or mystery writing—and I wonder about its source. I had not foreseen this ability nor contracted for its arrival. It seems simply to have appeared, perhaps from a source beyond myself. "A circulation of gifts nourishes those parts of our spirit that are not entirely personal," Hyde points out. "Although these wider spirits are a part of us, they are not 'ours'; they are endowments bestowed on us."

A second characteristic of gifts is paradoxical: gifts we receive are meant to be given away. What we receive is not meant only for private benefit. Blessings bestowed on us—talent, knowledge, prosperity—are not to be taken out of circulation or hoarded as ours alone. Instead, these gifts need to be handed on. As Hyde says, "The gift must always move." What good is a talent for singing if no one ever hears our song? What is the point of being a gifted scholar if our knowledge is not shared with others? If we keep a gift for our private enjoyment, it begins to wither; taken out of circulation, a gift loses its vitality. As Hyde observes, "A gift that cannot be given away ceases to be a gift. The spirit of the gift is kept alive by its constant donation."

The third characteristic is more curious still. Giving a gift creates a loss that is itself satisfying. Hyde writes, "A gift is property that perishes . . . a graceful perishing in which our hunger disappears as our gifts are consumed." In giving flowers, I surrender something beautiful to my friend. In that gesture I "lose" what I had earlier possessed. These flowers, for which I paid good money, are no longer mine; yet this loss is deeply satisfying. I am more than compensated by my friend's delighted smile. A similar dynamic takes place in sharing the gift of knowledge. The teacher "gives away" knowledge to students. But knowledge transmitted is not lost; it is multiplied. And the students' increased knowledge is matched by the teacher's increased satisfaction.

GRATITUDE AND GENEROSITY

A genuine gift brings us the delight of being cared for, even indulged. Such a gift reminds us of the mysterious and inexhaustible abundance available in the world. And we recognize our capacity to add to the world's wealth by being generous. A curious economics is at play here: we do not have to cling to what we have; gift-giving enlarges and enriches our own lives.

Gift-giving establishes ties between the one who gives and the one who receives, as gratitude links us to those who have blessed our lives. Paradoxically, then, there are no "free gifts," since these exchanges draw us into intricate webs of belonging and obligation.

The complicated patterns of reciprocity that arise from gift-giving create relations at once precious and precarious.

A good gift links us to the giver, but not in bondage. Genuine gifts teach us instead that dependence is a healthy part of life. Freely given, gifts expand us and invite our generosity. False gifts, on the other hand, bring not benefits but burdens and constraints. Secular and sacred literature are filled with stories of such treacherous, even fatal, gifts. In Homer's classic *The Iliad*, the Greek warriors fail to penetrate the fortress of Troy. Pretending to depart the battlefield, they leave behind the "gift" of a giant wooden horse. Hidden inside the figure of the horse are Greek soldiers who, once inside the city, will emerge to destroy their enemy. From this tale comes the warning, "Beware Greeks bearing gifts." In the Bible, we read of King Herod's promise to bestow upon Salome any gift she desires. The gift she demands, at her mother's instigation, is the beheading of John the Baptist.

Our everyday world includes gifts that can trap us in crippling indebtedness or demeaning dependency. Many gifts come "with strings attached." Such gifts carry hidden costs to the receiver; we accept them only to discover that we are now obligated to the giver. A colleague performs a favor for us, then quickly makes a far weightier demand. Family life too can involve gifts that have strings attached. Parents, after years of nurturing care, announce their hope that the young adult child will "make us proud." When the parents' plan for the child's future is resisted, the lament arises: "After all we've done for you . . . ." Now the gift's hidden contract and binding requirement are revealed.

America's culture of independence makes us suspicious even of the bonds that good gifts create. Personal autonomy and emotional independence are highly valued in this land. We do not want to be beholden to anyone; we like to pay our own way. As Ralph Waldo Emerson wrote over a century ago: "We cannot be bought or sold. . . . We wish to be self-contained." If this is our motto, surrendering to the healthy dependence of a gift exchange will be difficult. Personal history may deepen this cultural reluctance. Perhaps I have received gifts that were used as bribes, enticing me to act against my own best interests or rewarding me for following someone else's wishes. Or perhaps I grew up in troubled family, where affection was as scarce as money or food, and I am haunted in adult life by a sharp sense of deprivation. This remembered scarcity cripples my soul; I dare not embrace the erotic rhythms of gratitude and generosity.

Sociologist Georg Simmel defines gratitude as "a moral memory that binds together those who have exchanged gifts." The gift exchange comes to completion in generosity. As infants, we float in a sea of gifts. Our first breath and all the care that follows are extravagant examples of the legacy of our benefactors. But even as we are grateful, we recognize that there are many gifts that we can never repay. What amount would repay our parents for the life they have bequeathed us? How can we compensate a teacher or mentor who guided our early growth? Who can determine the market value of loyal colleagues or the appropriate price of an abiding friendship? These are debts that we cannot—and need not—repay. Through these gracious experiences, the *eros* of gratitude is slowly transformed into a desire to "go and do likewise." Recognizing that our lives have been blessed with such countless donations, we are eager to become gift-givers ourselves. Generosity is the labor of gratitude.

A GIFT ECONOMY

The gift exchange follows its own rules, what we might call the economy of the gift. The market economy follows the law of supply and demand, with appropriate concern for profit and attention to the bottom line. This is the economy of daily life, with its dynamics of paying bills and worrying about mortgages, of insufficient wages and ever-rising costs.

While the market economy is always with us, we are familiar with the gift economy too. Often we donate our time or other resources without seeking financial recompense. We give money to our church, volunteer at our children's school, or freely offer our professional advice to help get a worthy project started. We donate blood at the local hospital, collect clothing for the family that has lost everything in a fire, and bring hot meals to those who are housebound. In these exchanges we are not buying or selling, but discovering a satisfaction unrelated to financial profit.

Both the market economy and the gift economy create abundance. The market provides incentive for the development of products that will benefit human life: farmers produce more crops; pharmaceutical companies invent more effective medicines; contractors build homes in underserved areas; inventors work on energy-saving devices. In the market economy, abundance is always moderated by scarcity. Nobel Laureate economist Paul Samuelson emphasizes this essential element of the market: "At the core of economics is the undeniable truth that we call the law of scarcity, which states that goods are scarce because there are not enough resources to produce all the goods that people want to consume." In our personal lives, we are constantly made aware of this scarcity: we do not have enough time, or energy, or money to accomplish our goals.

The market economy operates in a zero-sum world: What you spend, you lose. If you devote an hour to one activity, that hour is gone; now it cannot be used to do something else. If you spend your savings on one project, those funds are no longer available for anything else. In the economy of the gift, a different calculus is at work. Giving is a loss that enriches us. As Leigh Schmidt writes, "Gift practices nudge us away from the supply-side, production-oriented model of the market into the negotiable reciprocities of exchange and the uneven graces of lived experience." Above all, in the gift economy we learn that not everything can be commercialized or commodified. The most precious aspects of life—friendship, devotion, courage, compassion—resist the market mentality. Faith and fidelity are not for sale.

The market economy is necessarily focused on production and quantity. Requirements of increased profit demand greater productivity, which generates the job-related stress of accomplishing more in less time. The gift economy raises questions about quality: Does increased production lead to more humane lifestyles? Does greater wealth ensure more satisfying relationships? Questions of economic value (what is the product's price?) are balanced by questions of worth (how does this activity improve the quality of our lives?).

A society flourishes when these two economies are in balance. Then career choices are enriched by a sense of vocation and weekly paychecks are augmented by the sense of satisfaction that comes from worthwhile work. And making a living serves a larger purpose—making a life.

A great gift of *eros* is its power to turn us outward, moving us beyond narrow self-concern toward fuller and more generous lives. Christian faith first arose within the climate of a gift economy—Jesus' insistence on compassion and forgiveness, his devoted pursuit of the reign of God. Immersed as we are in the myriad forces of the market economy, Christians today struggle to remember that our deepest satisfaction comes not from buying and selling, but from a more generous impulse—the *eros* of the gift.

How are we to reconnect with the generosity and fulfillment that flow in the gift exchange? A modest step may be to reawaken and cultivate the ordinary pathways of *eros*—surges of curiosity, movements of compassion, even the longings that accompany suffering and solitude. This will require us to find—or create—"holding environments," communities in which we revisit the gospel stories that tutor us in the rhythms of *eros*. Carving out space for gratitude and generosity, rescuing times for appreciation and celebration, we awaken our hope. And, enlivened by the *eros* of hope, we live even now in the promise of abundant life.

REFLECTIVE EXERCISE

Recall a recent gift-exchange in your own experience. Take time to settle again into the circumstances of this event—the persons involved, the occasion, the responses.

Then consider these questions:

What gift was exchanged here?

Were you the giver or the receiver or both?

What place did gratitude have in this experience?

What role did generosity play in this experience?

Additional Resources

Complete reference information for these resources can be found in the bibliography at the end of this book.

1. Naming Eros: Claiming the Energies of Life

Theologian James Nelson has written widely and well on a wide range of themes related to *eros* and Christian life. In this chapter we quote from his essay "Love, Power, and Justice in Sexual Ethics," in *Christian Ethics*, p. 288. The quotation from Andrew Solomon appears on p. 443 of his book, *The Noonday Demon*, as well as in his essay "A Bitter Pill."

On Gregory of Nyssa, see Peter Black's "The Broken Wings of Eros: Christian Ethics and the Denial of Desire," p. 110. Philip Sheldrake comments on Pseudo-Dionysius's use of *eros* in *Befriending Our Desires*, p. 45. Anders Nygren's *Agape and Eros* was originally published in Sweden in the 1930s; Philip Watson's English translation appeared in 1953. The-ologian Sallie McFague describes Nygren's view of *eros* and *agape* in her *Models of God*, p. 205, note 16. Also see Martin D'Arcy, *The Mind and Heart of Love: Lion and Unicorn—A Study of Eros and Agape*. In *Eros To-ward the World: Paul Tillich and Theology of the Erotic*, Alexander Irwin discusses Tillich's theology of *eros* and the subsequent critique of his po-sition that emerged among Protestant women theologians.

Poet Audre Lorde offered an early challenge to recover the metaphor of *eros* in her provocative essay "Uses of the Erotic: Erotic as Power."

Anne Bathurst Gilson provides her definition of *eros* in *Eros Breaking Free*, p. 110. Noelle Oxenhandler's comments are drawn from her essay "The Eros of Parenthood." Also see Martha Nussbaum's essay "Eros and the Wise: The Stoic Response to a Cultural Dilemma."

185

Pope Benedict XVI's encyclical letter, *Deus Caritas Est* (God Is Love) may be found at the Vatican website, <www.vatican.va>. Charles Taylor's comment appears in *A Secular Age*, p. 767. Andre LaCocque discusses the Song of Songs in "The Shalamite" in *Thinking Biblically*, pp. 236 and 263.

In *Power and the Spirit of God: Toward an Experience-Based Pneumatology*, Bernard Cooke explores a theology of the Spirit of God rooted in human experiences of power, nature, *eros*, and love. Donal Dorr examines the *eros* of God in *Divine Energy: God Beyond Us, Within Us, Among Us*.

2. Naming Grace: Receiving God's Blessing and Favor

We are especially grateful to Catherine Hilkert for the phrase "naming grace," which she develops in *Naming Grace: Preaching and the Sacramental Imagination*. Robert Ludwig offers an effective introduction to a Catholic understanding of grace in the chapter "The Experience of Grace" in his *Reconstructing Catholicism for a New Generation*. See also the work of Stephen Duffy in *The Graced Horizon: Nature and Grace in Modern Catholic Thought*.

For Plutarch's discussion of marital love, see his "Dialogue on Love," in *On Love, the Family, and the Good Life: Selected Essays of Plutarch*. Peter Brown comments on Plutarch in his masterful study, *The Body and Society: Men, Women, and Sexual Renunciation in Early Christianity*; we quote from p. 133.

Xavier Leon-Dufour discusses the extravagance of God's grace in his *Dictionary of Biblical Theology*; see especially pp. 218–19. Michael Skelley describes Karl Rahner's vision of grace in *The Liturgy of the World: Karl Rahner's Theology of Worship*, p. 60. For Rahner's own statement, see his "Considerations on the Active Role of the Person in the Sacramental Event."

3. Discovering Our God of Passion and Extravagance

Elizabeth Johnson provides one of the most significant contemporary restatements of a Christian theology of God in *She Who Is: The Mystery of God in Feminist Theological Discourse*. In her essay "God in Communion with Us," Catherine LaCugna examines the early theological controversies about God's nature and perfections. Kirsteen Kim discusses current cross-cultural theological contributions in *The Holy Spirit in the World: A Global Conversation.*

For Gregory of Nyssa's understanding of *eros,* see Peter Black's essay "The Broken Wings of Eros: Christian Ethics and the Denial of Desire"; we quote from p. 110. Astronomer George Coyne's observations on the immensity of the universe are found in Jim McDermott's interview, "The Fertile Universe."

Paul Ricoeur develops his ideas of "a logic of equivalence" and "a logic of superabundance" in *Figuring the Sacred,* p. 326; he examines Paul's "rhetoric of excess" in *Thinking Biblically,* p. 116. David Ford describes "a rhetoric of abundance" in Paul's writings in *Self and Salvation,* p. 113.

Philip Sheldrake demonstrates how our understanding of God shapes— and misshapes—Christian practice; see his *Spirituality and Theology: Christian Living and the Doctrine of God.* In *If God Is Love: Rediscovering Grace in an Ungracious World,* Philip Gulley and James Mulholland explore the personal and social implications of living out this biblical image of God.

4. A Spirituality of Eros: Praying for Our Heart's Desire

Theologian Wendy Farley provides a compelling reappraisal of the role of desire in *The Wounding and Healing of Desire;* we quote from pp. xii, 14, 31, and 83. In *The Transformation of Desire,* Diarmuid O'Murchu examines "how desire became corrupted—and how we can reclaim it."

In *The Holy Longing: Search for a Christian Spirituality,* Ronald Rolheiser traces links between *eros* and desire; we quote from p. 7. Philip Sheldrake explores spirituality and desire in *Befriending Our Desires;* we quote from p. 29. Psychiatrist Mark Epstein provides a contemporary appreciation of Buddhist insight into desire in *Open to Desire: The Truth about What the Buddha Taught;* we quote from p. 9.

As seasoned spiritual directors, Wilkie Au and Noreen Cannon Au draw on the Ignatian tradition to provide theological insight and pastoral guidance in *The Discerning Heart: Exploring the Christian Path.* In *The Sevenfold Yes: Affirming the Goodness of Our Deepest Desires,* Willi Lambert makes key aspects of Ignatian spirituality available for seekers of all faiths.

Michael Ignatieff's discussion of needs can be found in *The Needs of Strangers.* Charles Bouchard comments on the shift from desire to duty in "Recovering the Gifts of the Spirit in Moral Theology." We quote

James Nelson from "Love, Power, and Justice in Sexual Ethics" in *Christian Ethics*, pp. 288–89, and from p. 179 in Ron Hansen's novel *Mariette in Ecstasy*.

5. Eros in Everyday Life: Sensuality, Emotion, Sexuality

In *Honoring the Body: Meditations on a Christian Practice*, Stephanie Paulsell gives thoughtful consideration to the body as source and focus of Christian spirituality; see especially "Honoring the Sexual Body" and "Honoring the Suffering Body." Fran Ferder and John Heagle bring together the psychological and spiritual dimensions of sexuality in *Tender Fires: The Spiritual Promise of Sexuality*.

Erik Erikson discusses mature sexuality in many of his significant books; we quote from *Identity: Youth and Crisis*, p. 137. Roland Murphy's essay on the Song of Songs is found in *The Jerome Biblical Commentary*; we quote from p. 507.

In *Practicing Christianity: Critical Perspectives for an Embodied Spirituality*, Margaret Miles examines spiritual practices across Christian history for insight into the problem and the hope that such practices offer to today's world. We present an expanded discussion of embodied spirituality and sexuality in our book *Wisdom of the Body: Making Sense of Our Sexuality*.

We are grateful to our colleague and friend Mary Ann Finch for the reflective exercises we have adapted for use in this chapter, and in chapters 6 and 7. Mary Ann is known to many through her educational and formational ministry in the setting of the Graduate Theological Union in Berkeley and elsewhere. Over the past decade she has developed the Care Through Touch Institute, committed to providing caring touch and related ministries for those who are homeless and socially marginalized in the Tenderloin district of San Francisco. To learn more about this unique ministry, now expanding in new directions, contact Mary Ann Finch at Care Through Touch Institute, P.O. Box 420427, San Francisco, CA 94142.

6. Benefits of the Body: Storehouse of Wisdom and Energy

In *Calm Energy: Managing Energy, Tension, and Stress*, Robert Thayer examines energy and stress in their relation to human well-being; his earlier book, *The Origin of Everyday Moods*, is also helpful.

Luke Timothy Johnson's observation appears in his essay, "A Disembodied 'Theology of the Body': John Paul II on Love, Sex and Pleasure." We quote from p. 19 of Charles Frazier's novel *Cold Mountain*. Chinese scholar Ci Jiwei discusses the body's response to social trauma in *Dialectic of the Chinese Revolution;* we quote from p. 97.

Mihaly Csikszentmihalyi has written widely on the concept of "flow" and its implications in personal and social life; see especially *Finding Flow: The Psychology of Engagement in Everyday Life* and *Good Business: Where Excellence and Ethics Meet.*

In *Exuberance: The Passion for Life*, Kay Redfield Jamison examines positive resources of energy that emerge in our experiences of play, pleasure, creativity, spirituality, and joy. Michael Leunig's insightful reflections appear in his *Curly Pyjama Letters.*

7. Befriending Our Bodies: Lovely, Limited, Holy

In *Gospel Light: Jesus Stories for Spiritual Consciousness,* Jack Shea explores the role of the body along the journey of spiritual maturing. Carl Koch and Joyce Heil offer practical information about the body and suggestions for prayerful response in their *Created in God's Image.*

Mary Ann Finch provides sensitive practical guidance based on her pioneering exploration of the art of massage in holistic spirituality and holistic health, in *Care Through Touch: Massage as the Art of Anointing.* Christina Traina explores the sacramentality of the body in her essay, "Roman Catholic Resources for an Ethic of Sexuality," prepared for the Conference on Sexuality and Ethics sponsored by the *Catholic Common Ground Initiative;* this paper and other valuable resource materials are available online at <www.nplc.org/commonground/papers>.

In *Get Over Your Body and On With Your Life,* Rhonda Britten encourages women (and men) to overcome cultural pressures that make self-acceptance difficult. John Shekleton discusses memories of being an altar boy in his essay on the priesthood that appeared in *Commonweal.*

8. The Eros of Pleasure: Pathway to Presence and Gratitude

Augustine's reflections on food and pleasure can be found in *Confessions,* Book Ten. For a rich discussion of Augustine's difficulty with sensual pleasures, see Martha Nussbaum's *Upheavals of Thought: The Intelligence of Emotions.* Margaret Miles reflects on Augustine's *Confessions* in her *Desire and Delight: A New Reading of Augustine's Confessions.* James White examines Augustine's concern about the dangers of music in the liturgy in *Protestant Worship and Church Architecture;* we quote from p. 71.

Stella Resnick examines the broad scope of genuine pleasure in *The Pleasure Zone.* Jim Cotter discusses the disciplines of touch and the links between pleasure and fidelity in his essay "Homosexual and Holy" in the British spiritual journal *The Way.* C. S. Lewis's reflection on the spiritual significance of affection, pleasure, friendship, and love, *The Four Loves,* has become a classic; it continues to serve as a starting point for contemporary discussions of *eros* and *agape* in Christian life.

Celeste Snowber traces the legacy of embodiment in the Old and New Testaments in *Embodied Prayer: Toward Wholeness of Body, Mind, Soul.* In *Coming to Our Senses: Healing Ourselves and the World through Mindfulness,* Jon Kabat-Zinn suggests practices of meditation to assist in befriending the body. Thomas Ryan reviews historical and contemporary perspectives on the links between body and spiritual awareness and draws out social and ecological implications in *Reclaiming the Body in Christian Spirituality.*

9. Eros of Hope: Uninvited Envoy from Another World

Daniel Harrington draws on biblical images for a deeper appreciation of the resilient strength of hope; see *Why Do We Hope? Images in the Psalms* and *What Are We Hoping For? New Testament Images.* N. T. Wright explores the biblical narratives in *Surprised by Hope: Rethinking Heaven, the Resurrection, and the Mission of the Church.* Roberto Unger explores the ennobling passion of hope in *Passion: An Essay on Personality;* we quote from pp. 221, 244, and 238.

Paul Ricoeur examines the dynamics of hope in *Figuring the Sacred;* we quote from pp. 212 and 216. Ricoeur attributes to Soren Kierkegaard the comment that "hope is a passion for the possible." In *Theology of Hope,* Jürgen Moltmann describes the tension inherent in the Christian hope in the kingdom of God; we quote from p. 164.

In *The Anatomy of Hope: How People Prevail in the Face of Illness,* Jerome Groopman explores the links between hope and health; we quote from pp. xiv, 167, and 178. Abraham Verghese's article "Hope and Clarity: Is Optimism a Cure?" was originally published in the *New York Times*. In *The Psychology of Hope*, C. R. Snyder draws on current research in his discussion of the practical contribution of this positive emotion to personal well-being.

Adrienne Rich's poem "A Wild Patience Has Taken Me This Far" appears in her collection entitled *Poems 1978–1988*. Josef Pieper examines Aquinas's theology of patience in *The Four Cardinal Virtues;* see also Lee Yearley's discussion in *Mencius and Aquinas: Theories of Virtue and Conceptions of Courage.*

10. Eros of Suffering: Energy to Resist and to Accept

Wendy Farley offers profound reflections on suffering in *The Wounding and Healing of Desire* (we quote from p. 17) and in her earlier book *Eros for the Other* (we quote from p. 85). Martha Nussbaum explores the significance of suffering in *The Fragility of Goodness: Luck and Ethics in Greek Tragedy and Philosophy;* we quote from p. 390. David Tracy sketches a historical overview of theology's struggle to understand suffering in his essay "Evil, Suffering, Hope: The Search for New Forms of Contemporary Theodicy"; we quote from p. 18. In *Why Lord? Suffering and Evil in Black Theology*, Anthony Pinn examines the understanding of suffering that has emerged from the experience of African Americans.

In *Christ: The Experience of Jesus as Lord*, Edward Schillebeeckx examines the enormity of suffering; we quote from p. 724. Catherine Hilkert explores this further in her essay "Edward Schillebeeckx: Encountering God in a Secular and Suffering World"; we quote from p. 381.

In *Where Is God? Earthquake, Terrorism, Barbarity and Hope,* Jon Sobrino provides a moving examination of the reality and promise of hope in the face of suffering and injustice, rooted for Christians in an embrace of a deeper theology of the cross. Daniel Harrington draws on biblical insight in *Why Do We Suffer? A Scriptural Approach to the Human Condition.*

Anthony Tambasco brings together essays by theologians and biblical scholars to illumine the Bible's perspective; see *The Bible of Suffering: Social and Political Implications.* In *C. S. Lewis and Human Suffering*, Marie Conn traces the role of suffering in the life and work of this influential scholar and writer.

Eva Hoffman describes the heritage of suffering within her family in *After Such Knowledge*; we quote from pp. 34 and 54. See also the poignant account in *An Interrupted Life: The Diaries of Etty Hillesum*; Hillesum, a Dutch Jew, died in Auschwitz at the age of twenty-seven. Dietrich Bonhoeffer's reflection on suffering is found on p. 259 in James Woelfel, *Bonhoeffer's Theology: Classical and Revolutionary*.

John Makransky discusses the role of suffering in Buddhism in his essay "Buddhist Perspectives on Truth in Other Religions: Past and Present." Clifford Geertz examines religion's perspective on suffering in *The Interpretation of Cultures*; we quote from p. 104. The Marxist critique of religion appears in Karl Marx's introduction to his essay, "Contributions to the Critique of Hegel's Philosophy of Right," in *Marx, Early Writings*; we quote from p. 4. Ci Jiwei discusses the effects of unacknowledged trauma in *Dialectic of the Chinese Revolution*; we quote from p. 96.

11. Eros of Anger: Resource for Social Transformation

Beverly Wildung Harrison analyzes anger in her essay "The Place of Anger in the Works of Love," in *Making the Connections: Essays in Feminist Social Ethics*; we quote from p. 14. Dana Crowley Jack examines the emotion of anger in *Silencing the Self: Women and Depression*; we quote from p. 91.

Kathleen Fischer's *Transforming Fire: Women Using Anger Creatively* provides a spiritual perspective on anger's positive potential. See also our discussion of anger and its transformation in *Shadows of the Heart: A Spirituality of the Painful Emotions*.

In his characteristically balanced style, psychiatrist Willard Gaylin acknowledges anger's volatile presence in American society; see his recent book *Hatred: The Psychological Descent into Violence* and his earlier *The Rage Within: Anger in Modern Life*. Kathryn Tanner offers a positive analysis of traditional Christian theology as a partner—rather than an obstacle—in the human struggle to understand and respond to the call for social justice in *The Politics of God: Christian Theologies and Social Justice*.

In *Anger: Wisdom for Cooling the Flames*, contemporary Buddhist monk Thich Nhat Hanh reflects on the Buddhist tradition's perennial wisdom in understanding anger. Pastoral theologian Avis Clendenen and biblical scholar Troy Martin explore the dynamics of the "forgiveness exchange" in *Forgiveness: Finding Freedom through Reconciliation*.

For Aristotle's discussion of anger, see *Nicomachean Ethics*, X, 1125b26–1126b10 in *The Basic Works of Aristotle*. Thomas Aquinas examines anger in Questions 46–48 in the first section of the second part (1a-IIae) of the *Summa Theologiae*.

12. Eros of Compassion: Passion's Bridge to Justice

In *Compassion: A Reflection on the Christian Life,* Henri Nouwen locates this virtue at the heart of the Christian vision. In *An Open Heart: Practicing Compassion in Everyday Life*, the Dalai Lama describes the everyday practices through which the Buddhist understanding of compassion shapes a generous heart. In *Ordinary Grace: An Examination of the Roots of Compassion, Altruism and Empathy*, Kathleen Brehony explores the psychological dimensions of these basic human capacities.

William Spohn examines the Bible's role in "tutoring the imagination" in his essay "Jesus and Christian Ethics." Phyllis Trible discusses the Hebrew terms for *compassion* and *womb* in *God and the Rhetoric of Sexuality*. John de Gruchy explores the biblical vision in *Reconciliation: Restoring Justice*; we quote from p. 202.

In *Globalization, Spirituality, and Justice: Navigating the Path to Peace*, Daniel Groody draws on the biblical worldview and contemporary theological discussion to demonstrate the integral role of faith and spirituality in the struggle for a more just social order.

Pope John Paul II discusses the virtue of solidarity in his 1987 pastoral letter *Sollicitudo Rei Socialis* (On the Social Concern of the Church). David Hollenbach expands on this ethical principle in *Modern Catholic Social Teaching: Commentaries and Interpretations*. Robert Schreiter reflects on the significance of Christ's death for a spirituality of universal solidarity in the face of worldwide poverty and violence; see *In Water and in Blood: A Spirituality of Solidarity and Hope*.

13. Presence and Absence: Honoring Light and Darkness

In *Lost in Wonder*, Esther de Waal explores "the spiritual art of attentiveness" that enables us to live more fully in the presence of God. Ronald Rolheiser offers guidance and encouragement in *Shattered Presence: Recovering a Felt Presence of God*. Thomas Moore honors the spiritual insight that emerges in absence in *Dark Nights of the Soul*.

The work of Chinese sage Xunzi is available in *Hsun Tzu: Basic Writings,* edited by Burton Watson: we quote from p. 90. Adam Phillips examines the dynamics of composure in *On Kissing, Tickling, and Being Bored.* Svetlana Boym discusses "hypochondria of the heart" in *The Future of Nostalgia.*

Elaine Scarry reflects *On Beauty and Being Just;* we quote from pp. 25 and 65. Theologian Susan Ross reinforces the connections between beauty and care in *Beauty of the Earth: Women, Sacramentality and Justice.* In *Beauty: The Invisible Embrace,* poet-theologian John O'Donohue explores the experience of beauty as source of "compassion, serenity and hope."

14. Holding On and Letting Go: Learning the Rules of Engagement

In *Crossing the Desert,* Robert Wicks returns to the testimony of the desert saints of early Christianity, to explore their insight into the spiritual movements of holding on and letting go. Kerry Walters draws on these prophetic and mystical traditions to guide the spiritual journey in *Soul Wilderness: A Desert Spirituality.* Kenneth Stevenson reflects on the power of detachment to nurture and sustain the spiritual journey in *Rooted in Detachment: Living the Transfiguration.*

Ethicist Margaret Farley, in *Personal Commitments: Beginning, Keeping, Changing,* offers trustworthy guidance for discerning the authentic demands of fidelity in adult commitments. In *A Secure Base: Parent-Child Attachment and Healthy Human Development,* psychologist John Bowlby explores the relevance of his influential theory to mature adult development.

Garrison Keillor reflects on his religious upbringing in *Lake Wobegon Days;* we quote from pp. 254 and 261. We also quote from Roberto Unger, *Passion: An Essay on Personality,* p. 111.

15. Feasting and Fasting: Nourishing the Spirit

In *Wisdom's Feast,* Susan Cole, Marian Ronan, and Hal Taussig have crafted a series of prayerful and inclusive celebrations to reflect the biblical images of wisdom as the feminine face of God. Bernard Lee explores the connection between God and *eros* in his essay, "The Appetite of God," in *Religious Experience and Process Theology;* see also his book *Jesus and the Metaphors of God.*

In *Feasting with God* Holly Whitcomb provides practical guidance, inviting us to celebrate the preparation and sharing of food as moments of spiritual awareness. In his book *Fasting*, Dag Tessore traces the historical roots of this long-cherished spiritual discipline; Thomas Ryan offers both theological reflection and practical advice in *The Sacred Art of Fasting*. We explore the rhythm of feasting and fasting as part of the discipline of *eros* in *Wisdom of the Body: Making Sense of Our Sexuality*.

16. Shadows of Eros: Vital Energy Gone Astray

Paul Ricoeur explores eroticism in his classic essay, "Wonder, Eroticism, and Enigma." David Mura's poignant comment is drawn from *A Male Grief: Notes on Pornography and Addiction;* we quote from p. 19.

William Schweiker discusses "saturated desires" in *Having: Property and Possessions in Religious and Social Life,* especially p. 110. Benjamin Barber challenges the excesses of the market economy in *Consumed: How Markets Corrupt*; Kenneth Himes discusses the moral dimensions in "Consumerism and Christian Ethics." Leigh Schmidt examines religion's role in "Practices of Exchange: From Market Culture to Gift Economy in the Interpretation of American Religion," in *Lived Religion*.

In *Common Fire: Leading Lives of Commitment in a Complex World*, Laurent Parks Daloz and Sharon Daloz Parks offer compelling case stories and reflections to support personal and social commitment to the common good. Ronald Sider offers an analysis of the causes of international poverty in the twenty-first century and practical recommendations for Christian response in *Rich Christians in an Age of Hunger*. In *Engaged Spirituality*, Joseph Nangle explores ways in which reflection on the social dimensions of the gospel can transform spiritual awareness. The Ministry of Money represents a broad-based Christian network committed to study and action rooted in a gospel vision of money; for more information see the website: <www.ministryofmoney.org>.

Conclusion: The Eros of the Gift

Lewis Hyde's evocative discussion is found in *The Gift: Imagination and the Erotic Life of Property*. In *The Real Wealth of Nations*, Riane Eisler speaks powerfully and practically to the challenges of "creating a caring economics."

Georg Simmel explores the significance of gratitude in his essay "Faithfulness and Gratitude." Robert Emmons provides a helpful summary of his significant research on the emotion of gratitude in *Thanks! How the New Science of Gratitude Can Make Your Life Happier*. In *Radical Gratitude*, Mary Jo Leddy offers a challenging and supportive reflection on the spiritual power of the emotion and virtue of gratitude.

Risto Saarinen explores an ecumenical theology of giving in *God and the Gift*. Walter Brueggemann invites communities of faith into deeper reflection on the gospel vision in *Prayers for a Privileged People*.

Bibliography

Aristotle. *Nicomachean Ethics*. In *The Basic Works of Aristotle*, edited by Richard McKeon. New York: Random House, 1941.

Au, Wilkie, and Noreen Cannon Au. *The Discerning Heart: Exploring the Christian Path*. New York: Paulist Press, 2006.

Barber, Benjamin. *Consumed: How Markets Corrupt*. New York: Norton, 2007.

Begley, Louis. *About Schmidt*. New York: Knopf, 1996.

Benedict XVI, Pope. *Deus Caritas Est* (God Is Love). <www.vatican.va>.

Black, Peter. "The Broken Wings of Eros: Christian Ethics and the Denial of Desire." *Theological Studies* 64 (2003): 106–26.

Bouchard, Charles. "Recovering the Gifts of the Spirit in Moral Theology." *Theological Studies* 63 (2002): 539–58.

Bowlby, John. *A Secure Base: Parent-Child Attachment and Healthy Human Development*. New York: Basic Books, 1988.

Boym, Svetlana. *The Future of Nostalgia*. New York: Basic Books, 2001.

Brehony, Kathleen. *Ordinary Grace: An Examination of the Roots of Compassion, Altruism and Empathy*. New York: Riverhead Books, 1999.

Britten, Rhonda. *Get Over Your Body and On With Your Life*. New York: Simon and Schuster, 2005.

Brown, Peter. *The Body and Society: Men, Women, and Sexual Renunciation in Early Christianity*. New York: Columbia University Press, 1988.

Brueggemann, Walter. *Prayers for a Privileged People*. Nashville: Abingdon Press, 2008.

Ci Jiwei. *Dialectic of the Chinese Revolution*. Stanford, CA: Stanford University Press, 1994.

Clendenen, Avis, and Troy Martin. *Forgiveness: Finding Freedom through Reconciliation*. New York: Crossroad, 2002.

Cole, Susan, Marian Ronan, and Hal Taussig. *Wisdom's Feast.* New York: Rowman and Littlefield, 1997.

Conn, Marie. *C. S. Lewis and Human Suffering.* Mahwah, NJ: Hidden Spring, 2008.

Cooke, Bernard. *Power and the Spirit of God: Toward an Experience-Based Pneumatology.* New York: Oxford University Press, 2005.

Cotter, Jim. "Homosexual and Holy." *The Way* (July 1988): 231–43.

Csikszentmihalyi, Mihaly. *Finding Flow: The Psychology of Engagement in Everyday Life.* New York: Basic Books, 1999.

———. *Good Business: Where Excellence and Ethics Meet.* New York: Penguin Books, 2004.

Dalai Lama. *An Open Heart: Practicing Compassion in Everyday Life.* Boston: Little, Brown, 2002.

Daloz, Laurent Parks, and Sharon Daloz Parks. *Common Fire: Leading Lives of Commitment in a Complex World.* Boston: Beacon Press, 1996.

D'Arcy, Martin. *The Mind and Heart of Love: Lion and Unicorn—A Study of Eros and Agape.* New York: Meridian Books, 1956.

de Gruchy, John. *Reconciliation: Restoring Justice.* Minneapolis: Augsburg Fortress, 2002.

de Waal, Esther. *Lost in Wonder: Rediscovering the Spiritual Art of Attentiveness.* Collegeville, MN: Liturgical Press, 2003.

Dorr, Donal. *Divine Energy: God Beyond Us, Within Us, Among Us.* Liguori, MO: Triumph Books, 1996.

Duffy, Stephen. *The Graced Horizon: Nature and Grace in Modern Catholic Thought.* Collegeville, MN: The Liturgical Press, 1992.

Eisler, Riane. *The Real Wealth of Nations: Creating a Caring Economics.* San Francisco: Berrett-Koehler, 2007.

Emmons, Robert. *Thanks! How the New Science of Gratitude Can Make Your Life Happier.* New York: Houghton Mifflin, 2007.

Epstein, Mark, *Open to Desire: The Truth about What the Buddha Taught.* New York: Gotham Books, 2005.

Erikson, Erik. *Identity: Youth and Crisis.* New York: Norton, 1980.

Farley, Margaret. *Personal Commitments: Beginning, Keeping, Changing.* San Francisco: Harper, 1983.

Farley, Wendy. *Eros for the Other.* University Park, PA: Penn State University Press, 1996.

———. *The Wounding and Healing of Desire.* Louisville, KY: Westminster John Knox Press, 2005.

Ferder, Fran, and John Heagle. *Tender Fires: The Spiritual Promise of Sexuality.* New York: Crossroad, 2002.

Finch, Mary Ann. *Care Through Touch: Massage as the Art of Anointing.* New York: Continuum, 2000.

Fischer, Kathleen. *Transforming Fire: Women Using Anger Creatively.* New York: Paulist Press, 1999.

Ford, David. *Self and Salvation.* Cambridge University Press, 1999.

Frazier, Charles. *Cold Mountain.* New York: Atlantic Monthly Press, 1997.

Gaylin, Willard. *Hatred: The Psychological Descent into Violence.* New York: Perseus Publishing, 2004.

———. *The Rage Within: Anger in Modern Life.* New York: Simon and Schuster, 1984.

Geertz, Clifford. *The Interpretation of Cultures.* New York: Basic Books, 1973.

Gilson, Anne Bathurst. *Eros Breaking Free.* Cleveland, OH: Pilgrim Press, 1995.

Groody, Daniel. *Globalization, Spirituality, and Justice: Navigating the Path to Peace.* Maryknoll, NY: Orbis Books, 2007.

Groopman, Jerome. *The Anatomy of Hope: How People Prevail in the Face of Illness.* New York: Random House, 2004.

Gulley, Philip, and James Mulholland. *If God Is Love: Rediscovering Grace in an Ungracious World.* San Francisco: Harper San Francisco, 2003.

Hansen, Ron. *Mariette in Ecstasy.* New York: Harper Collins, 1991.

Harrington, Daniel. *What Are We Hoping For? New Testament Images.* Collegeville, MN: Liturgical Press, 2006.

———. *Why Do We Hope? Images in the Psalms.* Collegeville, MN: Liturgical Press, 2008.

———. *Why Do We Suffer? Scriptural Approach to the Human Condition.* Chicago: Sheed and Ward, 2005.

Harrison, Beverly Wildung. "The Place of Anger in the Works of Love." In *Making the Connections. Essays in Feminist Social Ethics,* edited by Carol Robb, 3–21. Boston, MA: Beacon Press, 1985.

Hilkert, Catherine. *Naming Grace: Preaching and the Sacramental Imagination.* New York: Continuum, 2002.

———. "Edward Schillebeeckx: Encountering God in a Secular and Suffering World." *Theology Today* 62 (2005): 376–87.

Hillesum, Etty. *An Interrupted Life: The Diaries of Etty Hillesum, 1941–43.* New York: Washington Square Press, 1985.

Himes, Kenneth. "Consumerism and Christian Ethics." *Theological Studies* 68 (2007): 132–53.

Hoffman, Eva. *After Such Knowledge.* New York: Public Affairs Press, 2004.

Hollenbach, David, Kenneth R. Himes, Lisa Sowle Cahill, Charles E. Curran, and Thomas Shannon, eds. *Modern Catholic Social Teaching: Commentaries and Interpretations.* Washington, DC: Georgetown University Press, 2005.

Hsun Tzu: Basic Writings. Edited by Burton Watson. New York: Columbia University Press, 1963.

Hyde, Lewis. *The Gift: Imagination and the Erotic Life of Property.* New York: Random House, 1983.

Ignatieff, Michael. *The Needs of Strangers.* New York: Henry Holt, 1984.

Irwin, Alexander. *Eros Toward the World: Paul Tillich and the Theology of the Erotic.* New York: Wipf and Stock, 2004.

Jack, Dana Crowley. *Silencing the Self: Women and Depression.* Cambridge, MA: Harvard University Press, 1991.

Jamison, Kay Redfield. *Exuberance: The Passion for Life.* New York: Vintage Books, 2005.

John Paul II, Pope. *Sollicitudo Rei Socialis* (On the Social Concern of the Church). <www.vatican.va>.

Johnson, Elizabeth. *She Who Is: The Mystery of God in Feminist Theological Discourse.* New York: Crossroad, 2000.

Johnson, Luke Timothy. "A Disembodied 'Theology of the Body': John Paul II on Love, Sex and Pleasure." *Commonweal Magazine* (January 26, 2001): 11–17.

Kabat-Zinn, Jon. *Coming to Our Senses: Healing Ourselves and the World through Mindfulness.* New York: Hyperion Books, 2005.

Keillor, Garrison. *Lake Wobegon Days.* New York: Viking, 1985.

Kim, Kirsteen. *The Holy Spirit in the World: A Global Conversation.* Maryknoll, NY: Orbis Books, 2007.

Koch, Carl, and Joyce Heil. *Created in God's Image.* Winona, MN: St. Mary's Press, 1991.

LaCocque, Andre. "The Shalamite." In *Thinking Biblically*, edited by Andre LaCocque and Paul Ricoeur, 235–63. Chicago: University of Chicago Press, 1998.

LaCugna, Catherine. "God in Communion with Us." In *Freeing Theology: The Essentials of Theology in Feminist Perspective.* San Francisco: Harper San Francisco, 1993.

Lambert, Willi. *The Sevenfold Yes: Affirming the Goodness of Our Deepest Desires.* Notre Dame, IN: Ave Maria Press, 2005.

Leddy, Mary Jo. *Radical Gratitude*. Maryknoll, NY: Orbis Books, 2002.

Lee, Bernard. "The Appetite of God." In *Religious Experience and Process Theology*, edited by Harry James Cargas and Bernard Lee, 369–84. New York: Paulist Press, 1976.

———. *Jesus and Metaphors of God*. New York/Mahwah, NJ: Paulist Press, 1998.

Leon-Dufour, Xavier. *Dictionary of Biblical Theology*. New York: Crossroad, 1973.

Leunig, Michael. *Curly Pyjama Letters*. Camberwell, Victoria: Penguin Books, 2006.

Lewis, C. S. *The Four Loves*. New York: Harcourt Brace Jovanovich, 1960.

Lorde, Audre. "Uses of the Erotic: Erotic as Power." In *Sister Outsider*. Crossing Press, 1984.

Ludwig, Robert. "The Experience of Grace." In *Reconstructing Catholicism for a New Generation*. New York: Crossroad, 1995.

Makransky, John. "Buddhist Perspectives on Truth in Other Religions: Past and Present." *Theological Studies* 64 (2003): 334–61.

Marx, Karl. "Contributions to the Critique of Hegel's Philosophy of Right." In *Marx, Early Writings*, edited by T. B. Bottimore. New York: McGraw-Hill, 1963.

McDermott, Jim. "The Fertile Universe: An Interview with George V. Coyne, Former Director of the Vatican Observatory." *America Magazine* (October 23, 2006).

McFague, Sallie. *Models of God*. Philadelphia: Fortress Press, 1987.

McManus, Kathleen, "Suffering in the Theology of Edward Schillebeeckx." *Theological Studies* 60 (1999): 476–91.

Miles, Margaret. *Desire and Delight: A New Reading of Augustine's Confessions*. New York: Crossroad, 1992.

———. *Practicing Christianity: Critical Perspectives for an Embodied Spirituality*. New York: Wipf and Stock, 2006.

Ministry of Money: Exploring Money and Spirituality. 11315 Neelsville Church Road, Germantown, MD 20076. <www.ministryofmoney.org>

Moltmann. Jürgen. *Theology of Hope*. Minneapolis, MN: Fortress Press, 1993.

Moore, Thomas. *Dark Nights of the Soul*. New York: Gotham, 2005.

Mura, David. *A Male Grief: Notes on Pornography and Addiction*. Minneapolis, MN: Milkwood Editions, 1987.

Murphy, Roland. "Commentary on the Song of Songs." In *Jerome Biblical Commentary*, edited by Raymond Brown, Joseph Fitzmyer, and Roland Murphy. New York: Prentice-Hall, 1968.

Nangle, Joseph. *Engaged Spirituality: Faith Life in the Heart of the Empire*. Maryknoll, NY: Orbis Books, 2008.

Nelson, James. "Love, Power, and Justice in Sexual Ethics." In *Christian Ethics*, edited by Lisa Cahill and James Childress, 284–98. New York: Pilgrim Press, 1996.

Nhat Hanh, Thich. *Anger: Wisdom for Cooling the Flames*. New York: Penguin Putnam, 2002.

Nouwen, Henri, D. A. Morrison, and D. P. McNeill. *Compassion: A Reflection on the Christian Life*. Revised Edition. New York: Doubleday Publishing, 2006.

Nuland, Sherwin, *Wisdom of the Body*. New York: Knopf, 1997.

Nussbaum, Martha. *Cultivating Humanity*. Cambridge, MA: Harvard University Press, 1997.

———. "Eros and the Wise: The Stoic Response to a Cultural Dilemma." *Oxford Studies in Ancient Philosophy*. Oxford: Clarendon Press, 1995.

———. *The Fragility of Goodness: Luck and Ethics in Greek Tragedy and Philosophy*. Revised Edition. New York: Cambridge University Press, 2001.

———. *The Therapy of Desire*. Princeton, NJ: Princeton University Press, 1994.

———. *Upheavals of Thought: The Intelligence of Emotions*. New York: Cambridge University Press, 2001.

Nygren, Anders. *Agape and Eros*. Translated by Philip Watson. Philadelphia: Westminster Press, 1953.

O'Connor, Kathleen. *Lamentation and the Tears of the World*, Maryknoll, NY: Orbis Books 2002.

O'Donohue, John. *Beauty: The Invisible Embrace*. New York: Harper Collins, 2005.

O'Donovan, Leo, ed. *A World of Grace: An Introduction to the Themes and Foundations of Karl Rahner's Theology*. Washington, DC: Georgetown University Press, 1996.

O'Murchu, Diarmuid. *The Transformation of Desire*. Maryknoll, NY: Orbis Books, 2007.

Oxenhandler, Noelle. "The Eros of Parenthood." *The New Yorker Magazine* (February 19, 1996): 47–49.

Paulsell, Stephanie. *Honoring the Body: Meditations on a Christian Practice*. San Francisco, CA: Jossey-Bass, 2002.

Phillips, Adam. *On Kissing, Tickling, and Being Bored*. Cambridge, MA: Harvard University Press, 1993.

Pieper, Josef. *The Four Cardinal Virtues*. Notre Dame, IN: University of Notre Dame Press, 1966.

Pinn, Anthony. *Why Lord? Suffering and Evil in Black Theology*. New York: Continuum, 1995.

Plutarch. *On Love, the Family, and the Good Life: Selected Essays of Plutarch*. Translated by Moses Hadas. New York: Mentor Books, 1957.

Rahner, Karl. "Considerations on the Active Role of the Person in the Sacramental Event." In *Theological Investigations* XIV, 161–80. New York: Seabury Press, 1976.

Resnick, Stella. *The Pleasure Zone*. Berkeley, CA: Conari Press, 1997.

Rich, Adrienne. "A Wild Patience Has Taken Me This Far." In *Poems 1978–1988*. New York: Norton, 1991.

Ricoeur, Paul. *Figuring the Sacred*. Minneapolis: Augsburg Fortress, 1995.

———. "Thou Shalt Not Kill: A Loving Obedience." In *Thinking Biblically*, by Andre LaCocque and Paul Ricoeur. Chicago: University of Chicago Press, 1998.

———. "Wonder, Eroticism, and Enigma." *Cross Currents* (Spring 1964): 133–41.

Rigali, Norbert. "From 'Moral Theology' to the 'Theology of Christian Life': An Overview." *Origins* (June 24, 2004): 85–91.

Rolheiser, Ronald. *The Holy Longing: Search for a Christian Spirituality*. New York: Doubleday, 1999.

———. *Shattered Presence: Recovering a Felt Presence of God*. New York/Mahwah, NJ: Paulist Press, 2006.

Ross, Susan. *Beauty of the Earth: Women, Sacramentality and Justice*. New York/Mahwah, NJ: Paulist Press, 2006.

Ryan, Thomas, ed. *Reclaiming the Body in Christian Spirituality*. New York/Mahwah, NJ: Paulist Press, 2005.

———. *The Sacred Art of Fasting: Beginning to Practice*. New York: Sky Light Paths, 2005.

Saarinen, Risto. *God and the Gift*. Collegeville, MN: Liturgical Press, 2005.

Scarry, Elaine. *On Beauty and Being Just*. Princeton, NJ: Princeton University Press, 1999.

Schillebeeckx, Edward. *Christ: The Experience of Jesus as Lord*. New York: Crossroad, 1983.

Schmidt, Leigh. "Practices of Exchange: From Market Culture to Gift Economy in the Interpretation of American Religion." In *Lived*

Religion, edited by David Hall, 69–91. Princeton, NJ: Princeton University Press, 1997.

Schreiter, Robert. *In Water and in Blood: A Spirituality of Solidarity and Hope*. Revised Edition. Maryknoll, NY: Orbis Books, 2007.

Schweiker, William, and C. Mathewes, eds. *Having: Property and Possessions in Religious and Social Life*. Grand Rapids, MI: Eerdsman, 2004.

Shea, Jack. *Gospel Light: Jesus Stories for Spiritual Consciousness*. New York: Crossroad, 1998.

Shekleton, John. "Homosexuality and the Priesthood." *Commonweal* (November 22, 1996): 15–18.

Sheldrake, Philip. *Befriending Our Desires*. Ottawa, CA: Novalis, 2001.

———. *Spirituality and Theology: Christian Living and the Doctrine of God*. Maryknoll, NY: Orbis Books, 2000.

Sider, Ronald J. *Rich Christians in an Age of Hunger*. New York: Thomas Nelson, 2005.

Simmel, Georg. *The Sociology of Georg Simmel*. New York: Free Press, 1950.

Skelley, Michael. *The Liturgy of the World: Karl Rahner's Theology of Worship*. Collegeville, MN: The Liturgical Press, 1991.

Snowber, Celeste. *Embodied Prayer: Toward Wholeness of Body, Mind, Soul*. Kelowna, Canada: Northstone, 2004.

Snyder, C. R. *The Psychology of Hope*. New York: Free Press, 2003.

Sobrino, Jon. *Where Is God? Earthquake, Terrorism, Barbarity and Hope*. Maryknoll, NY: Orbis Books, 2005.

Solomon, Andrew. "A Bitter Pill." *New York Times* (March 29, 2004): 18.

———. *The Noonday Demon*, New York: Scribner, 2001.

Spohn, William. "Jesus and Christian Ethics." *Theological Studies* 56 (1995): 92–107.

Stevenson, Kenneth. *Rooted in Detachment: Living the Transfiguration*. Collegeville, MN: Liturgical Press, 2007.

Tambasco, Anthony, ed. *The Bible of Suffering: Social and Political Implications*. New York/Mahwah, NJ: Paulist Press, 2002.

Tanner, Katheryn. *The Politics of God: Christian Theologies and Social Justice*. Minneapolis: Fortress Press, 2000.

Taylor, Charles. *A Secular Age*. Cambridge, MA: Harvard University Press, 2007.

Tessore, Dag. *Fasting*. Hyde Park, NY: New City Press, 2008.

Tetlow, Joseph. *Choosing Christ in the World*. St. Louis, MO: The Institute of Jesuit Sources, 1989.

Thayer, Robert. *Calm Energy: Managing Energy, Tension and Stress.* New York: Oxford University Press, 2003.

———. *The Origin of Everyday Moods.* New York: Oxford University Press, 1996.

Tracy, David. "Evil, Suffering, Hope: The Search for New Forms of Contemporary Theodicy." *Catholic Theological Society Proceedings* 50 (1995): 15–36.

Traina, Christina. "Roman Catholic Resources for an Ethic of Sexuality." *Common Ground,* March 5–7, 2004; paper available through <www.nplc.org/commonground/papers/trainapaper>.

Trible, Phyllis. *God and the Rhetoric of Sexuality.* Minneapolis: Augsburg Fortress, 1986.

Unger, Roberto. *Passion: An Essay on Personality,* New York: Free Press, 1984.

Verghese, Abraham. "Hope and Clarity: Is Optimism A Cure?" *New York Times* (February 22, 2004): 11–12.

Walters, Kerry. *Soul Wilderness: A Desert Spirituality.* New York/Mahwah, NJ: Paulist Press, 2001.

Whitcomb, Holly W. *Feasting with God.* New York: Pilgrim Press, 1996.

White, James. *Protestant Worship and Church Architecture.* New York: Oxford University Press, 1964.

Whitehead, Evelyn Eaton, and James D. Whitehead. *Shadows of the Heart: A Spirituality of the Painful Emotions.* Omaha, NB: iUniverse.com, 2004.

———. *Wisdom of the Body: Making Sense of Our Sexuality.* New York: Crossroad, 2002.

Wicks, Robert J. *Crossing the Desert.* Notre Dame, IN: Ave Maria Press, 2007.

Wilson, Walter. "Sin as Sex and Sex as Sin: The Anthropology of James 1:12-15." *Harvard Theological Review* 95 (2002): 147–68.

Woelfel, James. *Bonhoeffer's Theology: Classical and Revolutionary.* Nashville, TN: Abingdon Press, 1970.

Woodman, Marion. "Worshipping Illusions: An Interview with Marion Woodman." *Parabola* (May, 1987): 56–67.

Wright, N. T. *Surprised by Hope: Rethinking Heaven, the Resurrection, and the Mission of the Church.* New York: HarperCollins, 2008.

Yearley, Lee. *Mencius and Aquinas: Theories of Virtue and Conceptions of Courage.* Albany, NY: State University of New York Press, 1990.

Index

Abba, 30, 131

About Schmidt (Louis Begley), 100

absence, 172; befriending, 150, 151; generous, 149, 150; and presence, 144–51

abundance and gift economy, 182. *See also* extravagance

acupuncture, 67

addiction, 172

addictive behavior, 166

adolescence and body image, 79, 80

adulthood, emerging, 80, 81

adults, midlife, and physique anxiety, 81

Aeschylus on suffering and heroic deeds, 111

affection, 25, 26

After Such Knowledge (Eva Hoffman), 116

agape: and *eros*, 12, 14, 15, 25, 34, 35; in New Testament, 14

aging, 81, 82; befriending one's, 82, 83; physical changes of, 82

Anatomy of Hope, The (Jerome Groopman), 102

anger, 58; and *eros*, 119, 120, 121, 123, 124; and forgiveness, 125–28; holy, in the Bible, 119, 120; human, at God, 48, 49; and injustice, 122–24; moderating, 125; and relationships, 124–25; remembering, 123

Anselm on God as compassionate and passionless, 32

Aristotle: on anger, 121; on the common good, 137

Armstrong, Karen, on justice and compassion, 136

attachment and detachment, 158–59

Augustine, 14, 170; on desire, 45; on desire for God, 48, 49; on God, 32; and longing, 10; on pleasure, 90

Beaudoin, Tom, 175

beauty, 149

Begley, Louis, 100

Bellow, Saul, 93

Benedict XVI: on *eros*, 15, 16; on *eros* as God's love, 5, 35; on human and divine love, 15

Bible: and *eros*, 11; and justice, 137; sexual imagery in, 12, 13, 61, 62

biofeedback, 125

Black, Peter, on sins against *eros*, 175

blessing and grace, 20–22

body: estrangement from, 66; human, 64–74; instrumental, 85; and morality, 65; ornamental, 83–85, 86; sacramental, 86–87; wisdom of, 65

body image: development of, 77–83; and shame, 79

Bonhoeffer, Dietrich, on suffering, 117

breathing, mindful, 73

Brown, Peter, on grace of marriage, 26

Buddha and suffering, 108–9

Calvin, John, 14

catharsis, 111

caution, excessive, 170

celibacy, 162, 165

ch'i as vital energy, 66

charis, 24, 26; erotic nuance of, 26

charisma, 24

chastity, 166

Christ, presence of, 147

Ci Jiwei: on body and morality, 65; and traumatic suffering, 117

Cicero, 36

civic life, 173

Clement of Alexandria: on desire, 45; on pursuit of pleasure, 90

Cold Mountain (Charles Frazier), 64

commitment, 158, 159

common good, 137

compassion, 58; and *eros*, 131, 132, 170, 171; development of, 133, 134; failure of, 134–35; and justice, 135–37; and kinship, 133

composure, 148, 149

conflict: embracing, 155–57; in life and message of Jesus, 157; between Peter and Paul, 157; responses to, 156

consumerism, 174–75; and Christian values, 174

Cotter, Jim: on *eros* and fidelity, 26; on touching, 94

Council of Trent and legalism in spirituality, 46

courage and patience, 103, 104

creation and pleasure, 89, 90

Csikszentmihalyi, Mihaly, on flow of calm energy, 69

curiosity, 149; and *eros*, 169–70

D'Arcy, Martin, on erotic love, 15

depression, 162, 170; and vitality, 10

desire(s), 42–49; authentic, 46; God's, 47; and God's will, 42; human, and will of God, 47; influence of communities of faith on, 49; as lust in New Testament, 45; sinful reputation of, 45, 46; and spirit-flesh dualism, 44, 45; trusting one's, 44–48; unrequited, 48–49

despair and hope, 102

detachment, spirituality of, 158

Deus Caritas Est (Benedict XVI), 15

devotion, 58

Dialogue on Love (Plutarch), 24, 25

dieting, 79

economy, gift and market, 181–83

Emerson, Ralph Waldo, 180

emotions, 57–59

empathy, 57

energy, 66, 67; calm, 67, 69, 70; and exercise, 72, 73; flow of, 68; tense, 68, 70–71

Epstein, Mark, on desire, 43

equality, 35, 36

equivalence, logic of, 35, 36

Erikson, Erik, 115; on sexual passion, 59

eros: and absence, 48; and *agape*, 5, 12, 14, 15, 25, 5, 34, 35; and anger, 119, 120, 121, 123, 124; in the Bible, 11; and children, 53, 54; and closeness, 10; and compassion, 131, 132, 170, 171; and curiosity, 169–70; and desire, 11; divorce of, from grace, 27, 28; of the gift, 183; as god in ancient Greece, 9, 11, 14; and grace, 24–28; and Greek creation stories, 11; in Gregory of Nyssa, 14, 34, 35; and hope, 99, 100; and longing, 10; meanings of, 16, 17, 25; in Origen, 14; and pleasure, 25, 171–72; potential for destruction in, 168; in Proverbs, 11; in Pseudo-Dionysius, 14; rhythmic flow of, 143, 144; and sexuality, 16, 25, 59–60, 61, 62; sins of and against, 175; and social emotions, 59; in Song of Songs, 61, 62; and suffering, 108, 117; virtues growing from, 25; as vital energy, 9–11, 17, 20, 42, 53, 54; and vitality, 10, 17

eroticism, 172–73

Eucharist and presence of Christ, 147

exercise, 72, 73, 74, 85, 125

extravagance: biblical, 36, 37, 38; God of, 34, 35

faith community, 1

Farley, Wendy, on desire, 49, 175

fasting, 164–66; and Christian tradition, 162; communal, 165; in Eastern and Western Christian traditions, 164; as exercise of concentration, 164; and sexual life, 165; as spiritual discipline, 166

feasting, 162, 163; in biblical tradition, 161–62; as communal act, 163; and the senses, 163, 164; and sexual intimacy, 163

fidelity, 25, 26, 58

finding favor, and grace, 22–24, 27, 177

flow and energy, 68, 69, 70

forgiveness: and anger, 125–28; Jesus' call to, 128–29

Four Loves, The (C. S. Lewis), 94

Frazier, Charles, 64

freedom of assembly, 136

freedom of religion, 136

Geertz, Clifford, on suffering, 110

generosity, 94, 179–81

Gift, The (Lewis Hyde), 178

gift-giving, 179, 180

gifts, 178, 179, 180, 181

Gilson, Anne Bathurst, on *eros*, 16

God: as *Abba*, 131; absence of, 146; biblical convictions about, 30–31; desire and will of, 47;

in Eastern Christianity, 32; as
Emmanuel (God-with-us), 30;
experience of, 22; gifts of, 24,
177; of life, 9; as Lord of extravagance, 34, 35; as "other,"
139, 145; passionate, 31, 32;
as philosophical deity, 32; presence of, 145–47; and pleasure,
93; reign of, 105–6, 137; as
Ruah (animating spirit), 30; as
Shekinah (faithful presence),
30; silence of, 151; in Western
Christianity, 32
gossip, 170
grace: as blessing, 20–22; divorce
of, from *eros*, 27, 28; and *eros*,
19, 20, 24–28; and finding
favor, 22–24, 27, 177; as
God's free gift, 177; as God's
presence, 20; and hope, 99;
meanings of, 19, 20, 177
gratification, 26, 27
gratitude, 58, 179–81; and pleasure, 94, 95
Groopman, Jerome, on hope and
recovery from illness, 102, 103
guilt, 58

habits of grace, 166
Hall, Donald, on addiction, 172
Hansen, Ron, 47
Harrison, Beverly, on anger and
moral activity, 121
hearing, 55
Heil, Joyce, 85
Heilbrun, Carolyn, on midlife
women, 82
Heschel, Abraham, on God's
mood swings, 31
Himes, Michael, on divine pres-
ence as radical love, 5

Hoffman, Eva, on suffering, 116,
117
holding on: and letting go,
153–55, 159; and religious
faith, 154, 155
Holy Spirit, as ambassador of extravagance, 39, 40
Homer, 180
hope, 99, 100; celebrations of,
106–7; and despair, 102; as
eros, 99, 100; false, 101–2,
103; and God's reign, 105–6;
and grace, 99; medical perspectives on, 102–3; and past, present, and future, 100; patience
of, 103–5; and promise, 101
hot bath, 56, 74, 90
Hyde, Lewis, on gifts, 178, 179

Ignatieff, Michael, on needs of
the spirit, 43, 44
Ignatius of Loyola, 42
Iliad, The (Homer), 180
immigrants, 138
immune system, 65
injustice and anger, 122–24
intimacy and wrestling metaphor,
157
Irenaeus on full human person, 5
Isaiah (prophet) and feasting, 161

Jack, Dana Crowley, on anger,
122
Jesus: and call to forgiveness,
128–29; and feasting, 161, 162;
and justice, 135; and message
of abundance, 38, 39; and passion, 32, 33; and power of
touch, 56, 57; on sin and suffering, 114; suffering of, 109
Job and suffering, 113, 114

John of the Cross, sexual imagery in, 12
John Paul II, 84; on justice and solidarity, 137
Johnson, Luke Timothy, on sexuality and wisdom of the body, 65
Jung, Carl, on passions, 57
justice: and compassion, 135–37; and social well-being, 137; in Western social theory, 136

Karp, David, on aging, 81
Keillor, Garrison: on composure, 148, 149; on excessive caution, 170
kinship and compassion, 133
Koch, Carl, 85

LaCocque, Andre, on Song of Songs, 61
Lee, Bernard, on vision of final banquet, 161
legalism in spirituality, 46
Leon-Dufour, Xavier, on blessings of God, 21
Leunig, Michel, on tiredness, 69
Levinas, Emmanuel, and the "other," 138, 139
Lewis, C. S., 94
liberty, 136
life, losing one's, 144; right to, 136
liturgy: as feast, 163; and presence, 150
love: in Song of Songs, 12; spiritualizing of, 12; terms for, in New Testament, 13–15
Luther, Martin, 14

Mamet, David, on healing effect of drama, 111

Marcus Aurelius on the art of living, 156
Mariette in Ecstasy (Ron Hansen), 47
Marx, Karl, on suffering and religion, 111
massage, 56, 74, 91
McFague, Sallie, on eros and agape in Nygren, 15
meditation, 74, 125
Mencius: on compassion, 170; on life and death, 144; on suffering, 110
Miles, Margaret, on spiritual traditions of Western Christianity, 1, 2
misericordia, 132
molestation, sexual, 93, 94
Moltmann, Jürgen, on hope and God's reign, 105
Mura, David, on addiction, 172
Murphy, Roland, on Song of Songs, 61

needs, 43, 44; of the spirit, 43, 44; and wants, 44
neighbor, 133
Nelson, James: on desire, 46; on eros, 10
Noonday Demon (Andrew Solomon), 10
nostalgia, 148
Nussbaum, Martha, on healing without cure, 112
nutrition, 73, 85
Nygren, Anders, on human nature, 14, 15

optimism, 101, 102
ornamentation of the body, 83, 84, 85

"other," the, in the Bible, 138
Oxenhandler, Noelle, on *eros* in parenting, 16

pain and hope, 103
passion, sexual: development of, 60; and *eros,* 59–60, 62
patience, 103–5
Paul (apostle): and excess, 38; on grace, 24, 27, 177; and logic of equivalence, 35; on sin and death, 113; on the Spirit, 40; on suffering, 110, 111
Perl, Fritz, on pity, 135
philia in New Testament, 14
Phillips, Adam, on composure, 148
pity, 135
Plato, 26
pleasure(s), 171–72; and creation, 89, 90; divine, 89; and gratitude, 94; human, 89, 90; of need and appreciation, 94, 95; and presence, 90, 91, 92; sexual, 95; and the spiritual life, 89; suspicion of, 90
pleasuring, 95
Plutarch on *eros,* 24, 25, 26
pornography, 170, 173
prayer and silence of God, 151
presence: and absence, 144–51, 172; and pleasure, 92; practices of, 150, 151
privacy, right to, 136
Prometheus Bound (Aeschylus), 111
promise and hope, 101
punishment and suffering, 112–14

qigong, 67

Rahner, Karl: on grace and the world, 28; theological approach of, 5
religion: organized, 3; and ornamentation, 84
respect, 25, 26
Rich, Adrienne, on patience, 103
Ricoeur, Paul: on despair and hope, 102; on God's extravagance, 35; on sources of suffering in ancient world, 113; on tenderness, 172
rights, inalienable, 136
Rolheiser, Ronald, on spirituality and desire, 42

sacrament, body as, 86–87
Samuelson, Paul, on scarcity, 182
Scarey, Elaine, and beauty, 149
Schmidt, Leigh, on gift practices, 182
Schweiker, William, on consumerism, 174
senses, 54–56
sentimentality, 170–71
sex and sensuality in book of Ruth, 12–13
shame and body image, 79
Shekinah, 30, 146
Sheldrake, Philip, and human desires, 48
shibui, 83
sight, 54, 91, 95
Simmel, Georg, on gratitude, 181
sinfulness and suffering, 112–13
Skelley, Michael, on experience of God, 28
sleep, 74, 85
sleep-aids, 72, 74
smell, 55
Solomon, Andrew, 10

Song of Songs: and *eros*, 12; interpretation of, 61–62

Sophocles and story of suffering of Antigone, 111

Spirit as *ruah* (breath), 1

Spiritual Exercises (Ignatius of Loyola), 42

spiritual search, 3, 4, 5

spirituality: and being human, 3; and biblical tradition, 1; and Divine Mystery, 1, 4; and presence, 92, 93, 150; as response to God, 1; worldly, 2; and world's wisdom traditions, 2, 3

stress, 70, 71, 72

stress management, 74

suffering: ancient Greek understanding of, 111; and the Buddha, 108–9; and *eros*, 108, 117; of gods and humans in Greek writings, 111; and Jesus, 109; as punishment, 112–14; remembering, 117; saying "no"/"yes" to, 114–17; and sinfulness, 112–13; understanding, 110–12

Symposium, The (Plato), 26

tai chi, 66, 74

taste, 55, 56, 91, 93

Taylor, Charles, and *eros*, 5, 16

temper, 121

tenderness, 172, 173

tension, 67, 68

Teresa of Avila, sexual imagery in, 12

Tetlow, Joseph, on human desire and God's ambitions, 47

Thayer, Robert: on bodily rhythms, 67; on exercise programs, 74

theology, contemporary, characteristics of, 4, 5

Thomas Aquinas, 46; on anger, 121, 122; on courage and patience, 103, 104

Tillich, Paul, on erotic love, 15

tiredness, tense, 71–72

touch, 56, 91, 93

Tracy, David, on hope and apathy, 100

tragedy and suffering, 116

Traina, Cristina, on body and sacrament, 86, 87

trauma and suffering, 116, 117

Unger, Robert: on hope, 99, 107; on holding on and letting go, 153, 154

Verghese, Abraham, on false optimism, 103

virtues, 166

vitality and depression, 10

virginity, 162

voyeurism, 170

wants and needs, 44

"Wild Patience Has Taken Me This Far, A" (Adrienne Rich poem), 103

women: midlife, 81, 82; young adult, and body image, 80, 81; and fertility and parenthood, 81

Woodman, Marion, on addiction, 172

work, 173

Xunzi on preserving one's life, 144

yoga, 4, 125